Celebrate the Seasons

Celebrate the Seasons

with
Traditions and Recipes

Maurine R. Humphris

and

Patricia F. Hemming

Springville, Utah

ISBN: 1-55517-662-3
v.1

Published by Cedar Fort, Inc.
925 N. Main Springville, Ut., 84663
www.cedarfort.com

Distributed by:

Typeset by Marny K. Parkin
Cover design by Adam Ford
Cover design © 2002 by Lyle Mortimer

Printed in the United States of America
10 9 8 7 6 5 4 3 2 1

Printed on acid-free paper
Library of Congress Cataloging-in-Publication Data

Humphris, Maurine R.
 Celebrate the seasons with traditions and recipes / Maurine R.
Humphris and Patricia F. Hemming.
    p. cm.
 ISBN 1-55517-662-3
1. Cookery. 2. Entertaining. I. Hemming, Patricia F. II. Title.
TX714 .H85 2002
641.5--dc21
                                    2002010063

To our families—
the reason we celebrate

Contents

Preface

Every season hath its pleasures.

Thomas Moore

When we were young, the highlight of the day was coming home and opening the door to the smell of tempting dishes cooking. Mealtime was very special. So much of what we remember and cherish stays with us forever.

This book is filled with many of our favorite recipes and traditions that we have collected over the years from family and friends. We have had a wonderful time putting it together and remembering. As you read it, we hope you enjoy remembering, too.

Acknowledgments

For many hours of listening, encouraging, typing, reading, and supporting, we thank our families: Mike and Keely, Joe and Jon, and our friends Dean Ellen, Connie, and Toni.

And to those loved ones who gave us traditions, we express our gratitude.

January

Warming Trends

In a dream I saw them stand,
Hope and Memr'y, hand in hand:
Hope's sweet face was hid from view,
But I knew it pure and true.
Memr'y stood with tender gaze
Fixed upon the bygone days;
Wistful eyes but fair and clear,
All undimmed by shame or fear:
This I, dreaming, seemed to see;
This my New Year Prayer for thee.

G. P. Meade

Candles

Candlelight adds beauty and warmth to any occasion. It welcomes all who enter and beckons them to stay. Candlesticks or holders can help set the mood of the party; silver or brass are formal, whereas clear glass or ceramic are more casual. Arrange the candles in different ways—line candles of different heights on a mantel or low table. Place two long tapers on a dinner table or group several small votives down

1

the middle of the table. Place plumber candles in cored apples or votives in hollowed out lemons. Choose a different color for each occasion or combine a variety of sizes and colors. Remember that candlewicks should always be charred before the guests arrive, as a sign of hospitality.

Fun Tips

Ham found its way to spring tables by way of pre-refrigeration methods of food preservation. Hogs were butchered in the fall. Large cuts, such as the hind legs, took six months to cure—meaning they were ready to eat in the spring.

Winter Picnic

Chili (p. 66)

Tamales (purchased)

Malted Bread Sticks (p. 82) and Clam Dip (p. 152)

Carrot and Celery Strips

Snowballs (p. 109)

Date Cake (p. 116)

Leftover Christmas Cookies

Eskimo Punch (p. 191)

---

* Have a winter picnic on a blanket in front of a roaring fire in the fireplace.
* Toast marshmallows.
* Put a puzzle together.
* Watch a football game.
* Place New Year's resolutions in your Christmas stockings to read next December when you have the "Hang the stockings" ritual.
* Put the Christmas tree outside for the birds—leave the popcorn or cranberries on it.
* Make gingerbread cookies, sprinkle with bird seed, and watch the birds have a feast. Pine cones can also be "frosted" with peanut butter and sprinkled with bird seed.
* Share your favorite or funniest experience of the past year.
* Create a snow scene on construction paper using Ivory snowflakes.
* Make January a "good health" month; plan good-for-you snacks; try new vegetables; plan a fun indoor exercise routine.

Warming Trends

Casseroles

BRUNCH OMELET

8 eggs, beaten
½ cup milk
½ cup heavy cream
3 tablespoons mayonnaise
1 tablespoon flour
1 cup ham, chopped
1 cup shredded cheddar cheese
3 green onions, sliced

Grease square baking dish. Blend eggs, milk, cream, mayonnaise, and flour. Add ham, cheese, and onions. Pour into prepared dish. Bake uncovered at 325 degrees for 35 to 40 minutes or until omelet is set and top is golden brown.

Yield: 6 servings

ZUCCHINI AND SCALLION FRITTATA

2 cups unpeeled, diced zucchini
1 tablespoon butter or margarine
½ cup soft whole wheat bread crumbs
⅓ cup milk
¾ cup chopped scallions
6 eggs, beaten
⅓ cup grated Parmesan cheese
Salt and pepper (to taste)
Garnish with cherry tomato wedges

Sprinkle zucchini with salt and drain for 15 minutes; pat dry. Preheat oven to 350 degrees. Melt butter or margarine in a medium skillet. Add zucchini and sauté over medium heat 3 minutes. In a large bowl, combine bread crumbs and milk; let stand 5 minutes. Stir in cooked zucchini, scallions, and eggs; season with salt and pepper. Pour mixture into a buttered 9-inch pie plate; sprinkle with Parmesan cheese. Bake 25 minutes or until set. Cut into wedges. Garnish with tomato.

Yield: 6 servings

CHEESE STRATA

12 slices day-old bread
2½ cups milk
½ pound American cheese, thinly sliced
4 eggs, beaten
½ teaspoon dry mustard
1 tablespoon grated onion
1 teaspoon salt
Dash cayenne pepper
Paprika for garnish

Remove crusts from bread. Cut on the diagonal. Arrange 6 slices in greased baking dish. Cover bread with cheese slices, then remaining bread. Combine remaining ingredients and pour over bread. Sprinkle top with paprika, if desired. Let stand in refrigerator at least 1 hour. Bake in slow oven (325 degrees) about 40 minutes or until puffy and golden brown.

Yield: 6 servings

CHILI RELLENOS CASSEROLE

2 cans (4 ounces each) chiles
½ to ¾ pound Cheddar cheese, shredded
½ to ¾ pound Monterey Jack cheese, shredded
1 can (15 ounces) evaporated milk
4 eggs
Salt and pepper
Salsa

Butter oblong pan. Line with chilis. Add cheese. Beat eggs into milk. Pour over cheese, mix well. Bake at 350 degrees for 45 minutes.

Serve topped with salsa.

CHINESE HAYSTACKS

Creamed chicken mixture:

1 cup chicken broth
2 cans (10¾ ounces each) cream of chicken soup
2 cups diced cooked chicken

Stir chicken broth into chicken soup and heat thoroughly, stirring until smooth. Fold in chicken and heat again. This mixture may be frozen ahead of time.

Accompaniments:

8 cups cooked rice (2½ cups uncooked)
1 can (5 ounces) Chinese noodles
2 cans (20 ounces each) chunk pineapple, drained
2 cans mandarin oranges, drained
1 cup sliced green onions
1 cup chopped celery
1 cup chopped green pepper
1 cup diced fresh tomatoes
1 small jar pimentos, drained
1 cup coconut
½ cup slivered almonds

Heat the creamed chicken mixture and cook the rice; keep hot on serving table in crock pot or chafing dish. Place all the accompaniments in separate bowls around a serving counter or buffet table. Guests "build" their own haystacks by placing a bed of rice in the bottom of a small bowl, spoon on hot chicken mixture, then top with any or all of the accompaniments.

Yield: 15 to 20 servings

EASY LASAGNA

1 package lasagna noodles
1½ pounds ground beef
2 cans (8 ounces each) tomato sauce
1 cup water
1 package spaghetti sauce mix
½ teaspoon salt
½ teaspoon garlic salt
1 cup sour cream
3 tablespoons cottage cheese
1 package frozen chopped spinach, thawed and drained well
3 green onions, chopped
Grated Cheddar cheese or Mozzarella cheese

Cook noodles. Brown meat and add next 5 ingredients and simmer. Mix sour cream and cottage cheese. Layer meat, noodles, sour cream mixture, and spinach in baking dish. Sprinkle green onions over top and cover with grated Cheddar cheese. Bake at 350 degrees for 25 to 30 minutes. May be made ahead and refrigerated. Then let sit at room temperature for 1 hour and bake for 1 hour.

CASSEROLE IN A PUMPKIN SHELL

1 medium (8 to 10 inch) pumpkin or squash. Cut out lid as you would for jack-o'-lantern and clean out the inside. Put lid back on the pumpkin and place on cookie sheet. Bake at 350 degrees for 45 minutes. Pumpkin should remain firm. While baking, put together casserole mixture.

Casserole Mixture:

2 pounds ground beef
4 potatoes, cubed or grated
3 carrots, grated
1 medium onion, chopped
2 teaspoons salt
½ teaspoon oregano
1 teaspoon vinegar
⅓ cup chopped green olives (optional)
½ teaspoon pepper
¼ teaspoon garlic powder
1 can tomato soup
3 eggs, beaten

Brown ground beef. Add potatoes, carrots, and onion and cook until vegetables are tender. Mix spices, tomato soup, and eggs and blend together well. Pour over meat and vegetable mixture and mix together.

Pack into the pumpkin and with the lid on, return to the oven and bake at 350 degrees for 1 to 1½ hours. The last 20 minutes of baking, remove lid, stir well and continue baking without the lid on for the remaining 20 minutes.

Serve as a Halloween centerpiece. Place pumpkin on platter and serve with a ladle. A variety of fruits (grapes, apples, etc.) can be served around the pumpkin for a complete meal. When serving, scrape some of the pumpkin from the inside of the shell.

SALMON MOUSSE

1 can (15½ ounces) salmon
Cold water
2 envelopes unflavored gelatin
¼ cup lemon juice
½ cup peeled, seeded, and chopped cucumber
½ cup chopped onion
½ cup chopped celery
½ teaspoon salt
½ teaspoon dill weed
1 cup mayonnaise
1 cup heavy cream

Drain and flake salmon, reserving liquid. Add water to reserved liquid to equal 1 cup. Soften gelatin in liquid; heat over medium heat until dissolved. Pour mixture into food processor or blender container. Add lemon juice, chopped cucumber, onion, and celery. Process until well mixed. Add salt and dill weed.

Remove half of mixture; set aside. Add ½ cup of the mayonnaise and ½ cup of the cream to mixture in container; process. Remove from container. Repeat with remaining salmon mixture, mayonnaise, and cream. Combine and pour into lightly oiled (with mayonnaise) 6-cup mold. Chill until firm. Garnish with cucumber, lemon, and watercress, if desired.

Yield: 6 servings

IMPOSSIBLE CHEESEBURGER PIE

1 pound ground beef
1½ cups chopped onion
1½ cups milk
¾ cup baking mix (Bisquick)
3 eggs
½ teaspoon salt
¼ teaspoon pepper
2 tomatoes, sliced
1 cup shredded Cheddar cheese or processed American
   cheese

Heat oven to 400 degrees. Grease pie plate, 10x1½ inches. Cook and stir beef and onion over medium heat until beef is brown; drain. Spread in plate. Beat milk, baking mix, eggs, salt, and pepper until smooth, 15 seconds in blender on high or 1 minute with hand beater. Pour into plate. Bake 25 minutes. Top with tomatoes; sprinkle with cheese. Bake until knife inserted in center comes out clean, 5 to 8 minutes. Cool 5 minutes.

Yield: 6 to 8 servings

BAKED BEANS

1 can (31 ounces) pork-n'-beans
1 can (15 ounces) pork-n'-beans
½ pound bacon, fried crisp and crumbled
1 large onion, chopped and cooked until transparent
½ green pepper, chopped
2 tablespoons prepared mustard
1 cup catsup
2 tablespoons light molasses
2 tablespoons brown sugar

Mix above ingredients together. Bake at 300 degrees for 2 hours.

Note: Can be made ahead and reheated 1 hour before serving.

SLOPPY JOES

1 pound ground beef
½ medium green pepper (diced)
½ cup chopped onions
1 can chicken gumbo soup
3 tablespoons catsup
1 tablespoon prepared mustard

Brown beef, green pepper, and onions. Drain. Add soup, catsup, and mustard. Simmer for 20 minutes or until thick and "sloppy." Spoon onto buns and top with a slice of cheese, if desired.

Yield: 6 servings

"More"

2 cups uncooked macaroni
1 medium onion, chopped
2 tablespoons butter
1 pound ground beef
1 teaspoon salt
Pepper to taste
1 can (16 ounces) tomato sauce
1 can (11 ounces) whole kernel corn
    OR 1 package (10 ounces) frozen corn
½ pound grated cheddar cheese
Add dashes of taco sauce to meat mixture for spicier
    flavor

Cook macaroni until tender; rinse and drain. Brown onion in butter until golden. Add meat, salt, and pepper. Cook and stir until crumbly. Add tomato sauce and let simmer till mixture thickens. Layer in casserole dish with deep sides: macaroni, meat sauce, corn, and cheese. Repeat layers, ending with cheese. Bake at 350 degrees for 30 minutes or until bubbly and heated through.

Yield: 6 to 8 servings

BEEF CASSEROLE MEXICANA

1 pound ground beef
1 small onion, chopped
1 clove garlic, minced
1 can (10¾ ounces) condensed cream of mushroom
    soup
1 can (4 ounces) chopped green chilis
1 package (6¼ ounces) corn or tortilla chips
1 can (10 ounces) mild enchilada sauce
2 cups shredded Monterey Jack cheese

Crumble ground beef into 1-quart glass casserole; add onions and garlic. Microcook, uncovered, 5 to 6 minutes or until meat is set. Stir to break meat into pieces; drain fat. Stir in soup and chilis.

Layer ⅓ (about 2 cups) corn chips and half each of meat mixture, enchilada sauce, and cheese in 12x8-inch glass baking dish. Top with another third of corn chips and remaining meat mixture, enchilada sauce, and cheese. Sprinkle with remaining corn chips.

Microcook uncovered 10 to 12 minutes or until hot and bubbly.

Yield: 6 to 8 servings

VEGETABLE STROGANOFF

1 package (12 ounces) linguini, cooked
2 cups broccoli florets
2 cups sliced carrots
1 cup creamed cottage cheese
¾ cup sour cream
½ cup grated Parmesan cheese
1 medium onion, chopped
¼ pound mushrooms
3 tablespoons butter
2 tablespoons flour
1 teaspoon salt
¼ teaspoon pepper
2 cups milk
½ cup sliced olives

Cook broccoli and carrots until crisp and tender, drain. Combine cottage cheese, sour cream, and ¼ cup of Parmesan cheese.

Sauté onion and mushrooms in butter until tender. Stir in flour, salt, and pepper; cook until smooth and thickened. Add olives and vegetables, stir about 1 cup hot mixture into sour cream mixture; add to vegetable mixture. Heat thoroughly, do not boil. Add linguini, toss to mix. Serve with remaining Parmesan cheese.

Yield: 10 servings

GARDEN VEGETABLE STEW

2 tablespoons butter
1 cup sliced onions
4 small zucchini, diced
2 cups sliced cauliflower
3 medium tomatoes, wedged
1 green pepper, seeded and cubed
½ teaspoon basil leaves
1 teaspoon salt
½ teaspoon sugar
1 can (10¾ ounces) tomato soup
1 pound frankfurters, cut in fourths
½ cup bacon bits
    OR 6 slices cooked bacon, crumbled

In large bowl, microcook butter on High 30 seconds. Add onions. Cover with plastic wrap and microcook 1 minute, until onions are limp. Add zucchini, cauliflower, tomatoes, green pepper, basil, salt, and sugar. Mix well. Microcook on High 6 minutes, stirring after 3 minutes. Add soup and frankfurters. Microcook on High 5 minutes, stirring once to heat through. Top with bacon bits.

Yield: 6 servings

Do-It-Yourself Pizza

1 can (16 ounces) tomato sauce
1 cup coarsely chopped tomato
½ teaspoon oregano leaves
½ teaspoon basil leaves
2 packages (13¾ ounces each) hot roll mix

Assorted pizza toppings:
Grated cheese
Chopped pepper
Minced onion
Pepperoni
Hot dogs
Mushrooms

Heat tomato sauce, tomato, oregano, and ½ teaspoon basil to boiling; reduce heat and simmer uncovered 5 minutes. Cover 7-inch paper plates completely with foil, grease lightly.

Prepare roll mix according to package directions, but do not let dough rise. Divide dough into eight equal portions. Spoon sauce and toppings into bowls. Let children spread dough on plates to form pizza crusts. Spoon scant ¼ cup sauce on each and let children choose and sprinkle toppings on pizzas.

Place pizzas on cookie sheet. Bake at 375 degrees until crusts are golden, about 20 minutes. Let cool several minutes before serving.

Yield: Eight 7-inch pizzas

One-Meal Chicken Bake

1 package (16 ounces) frozen mixed broccoli, cauliflower, and carrots
1 can (10¾ ounces) cream of chicken soup
¾ cup milk
¼ teaspoon salt
¼ teaspoon pepper
2 cups cubed, cooked chicken
1 cup shredded Cheddar cheese
1 can (2.8 ounces) french–fried onions
1 cup biscuit mix
1 egg
¼ cup milk

Thaw and drain vegetables. Mix with soup, milk, salt, pepper, chicken, ½ cup cheese, and ½ can french-fried onions. Spread mixture in an oblong baking dish. Bake uncovered at 425 degrees for 10 minutes. Meanwhile, combine biscuit mix, egg, and milk to form a soft dough. Spoon over hot chicken mixture. Bake uncovered at 425 degrees for 20 to 25 minutes or until biscuits are golden brown. Top with remaining cheese and onions and bake an additional 3 to 5 minutes.

Yield: 6 servings

SAUERKRAUT SEIANKA

2 tablespoons oil
4 medium carrots, grated
3 medium onions, chopped
1 quart sauerkraut
6 to 8 frankfurters, thinly sliced
1 cup grated cheese

Combine oil, carrots, onions, and sauerkraut in a frying pan and cook about 5 minutes. Add frankfurters; place in a buttered 2-quart casserole and top with cheese. Bake at 300 degrees for 1 hour.

SLUM GULLION

½ pound ground beef
½ onion, chopped
1 can (26½ ounces) spaghetti
1 can (10¾ ounces) cream of mushroom soup
½ pound Cheddar cheese, shredded

Brown beef and onions; drain. Add spaghetti and soup and cook on low temperature until hot. Sprinkle with cheese just before serving.

Variation: 1 can of creamed corn can be added instead of soup.

Navajo Tacos

6 cups flour
3 tablespoons baking powder
¼ cup corn syrup
1 teaspoon salt
3 cups water

Mix all ingredients together and set aside for 20 minutes before frying. Roll tablespoon of dough in ball and roll in flour. Pat dough flat between hands. Fry in hot grease at 350 to 400 degrees.

Topping:

1 pound lean ground beef, browned and drained
1 can (15 ounces) chili
1 cup water
1 package (1.5 ounce) taco seasoning mix
Shredded lettuce
Shredded cheese
Chopped tomatoes
Sour cream

Add chili, taco seasoning, and water to meat. Simmer 10 to 15 minutes. Spread meat mixture on top of fry bread; top with tomatoes, cheese, lettuce, and sour cream.

Yield: 15 tacos

WILD RICE CASSEROLE

2 cups water
⅔ cup wild rice
1 can chicken and rice soup
1 can (4 ounces) mushroom pieces
½ cup water
1 teaspoon salt
⅛ teaspoon each celery salt, onion salt, garlic salt,
    pepper, and paprika
1 small bay leaf, crumbled
1 teaspoon Worcestershire sauce
3 tablespoons chopped onion
3 tablespoons bacon drippings or vegetable oil
¾ pound ground beef

Bring 2 cups water to a boil; add rice; cover, and let simmer 15 minutes. Rest 5 minutes. Drain rice; add the soup, mushrooms, ½ cup water, and all the seasonings. Sauté onions; add meat and cook until browned and crumbly. Stir into rice. Pour into a casserole dish and bake at 325 degrees for 1 hour.

Yield: 4 to 5 servings

Salmon Patties

1 cup salmon
¾ cup dry bread crumbs
¼ cup minced green pepper
1 egg, slightly beaten
¾ cup cream of celery soup

Combine all ingredients. Using ¼ cup of mixture for each, shape into patties. Place in a frying pan and brown on both sides over medium heat. Serve with tartar or CELERY SAUCE. (recipe follows)

Yield: 8 servings

Celery Sauce

¾ cup cream of celery soup
1 teaspoon prepared mustard
½ cup milk
1 tablespoon sweet pickle relish
1 hard cooked egg, chopped

Combine all ingredients and warm over low heat. Serve over salmon patties.

CRAB AND ARTICHOKE CASSEROLE

3 tablespoons butter
3 tablespoons flour
1 ½ cups milk
1 teaspoon salt
⅛ teaspoon pepper
1 teaspoon Worcestershire sauce
¼ teaspoon prepared mustard
1 can artichoke hearts
4 hard boiled eggs, peeled and quartered
2 cans crab
⅓ cup grated Swiss cheese

Melt butter in a saucepan; add flour and cook on medium temperature about 1 minute. Slowly add milk, stirring constantly until thickened. Add remaining ingredients, saving cheese for the topping. Place in a buttered 1½ quart casserole; sprinkle with cheese. Bake at 350 degrees for 30 minutes.

Yield: 4 to 6 servings

CHICKEN STUFFING CASSEROLE

1 box Stove Top stuffing mix with rice; prepared
    according to package directions using 1 cup water
2 to 3 cups cooked chicken, cut into bite-size pieces
1 can (10¾ ounces) cream of chicken soup
¼ cup milk
Chopped pimento and chopped parsley for garnish

Place stuffing in a buttered 1½ quart casserole dish, press-ing some of the stuffing up along the side of the casserole to create a hollow center. Arrange chicken in hollow area. Blend soup and milk; pour over chicken. Cover and bake at 350 degrees for 35 minutes. Garnish with pimento and pars-ley, if desired.

Yield: 4 to 5 servings

TURKETTI

1¼ cups uncooked spaghetti, broken into about
    2-inch pieces
1½ to 2 cups diced cooked turkey or chicken
¼ cup pimento
¼ green pepper, diced
½ small onion, chopped
1 can (10¾ ounces) cream of mushroom soup
½ cup turkey broth or water
½ teaspoon salt
⅛ teaspoon pepper
1¾ cups (½ pound) grated sharp cheddar cheese,
    divided

Cook spaghetti, drain and rinse well. Combine all ingredient, saving ½ cup cheese for topping. Place in a buttered casserole dish; top with cheese; bake at 350 degrees for 45 minutes to 1 hour, or until hot and bubbly.

Note: Can be made a day ahead and refrigerated.

CRAB BAKE IN SHELLS

2 cups crab meat
2 hard boiled eggs, chopped
½ cup buttered bread crumbs
1 teaspoon fresh parsley, chopped
2 teaspoons lemon juice
1 teaspoon grated onion
1 cup mayonnaise
3 tablespoons sherry
½ teaspoon Worcestershire sauce
½ teaspoon prepared mustard
½ cup buttered bread crumbs for topping

Mix all ingredients, except last ½ cup bread crumbs. Place in greased baking shells, cover with bread crumbs and bake at 400 degrees for 15 minutes.

Yield: 6 servings

CHEESE ENCHILADAS

2 tablespoons vegetable oil
1 can enchilada sauce
1 dozen corn tortillas
2 onions, chopped
1 can chopped olives
½ pound grated cheddar cheese
Chopped lettuce for garnish

Place oil and enchilada sauce in a frying pan and heat. Dip each tortilla in sauce for 30 seconds, then remove to a plate. Place one teaspoon each of onions, olives, and cheese on the center of the tortilla, then roll. Place close together in a buttered baking dish; pour remaining sauce over the top and sprinkle with remaining onions, olives, and cheese. Bake at 300 degrees for 5 minutes or until hot and cheese is melted. Garnish with chopped lettuce.

Yield: 6 servings

ALMOND–TUNA CASSEROLE

2 cans (10¾ ounces each) cream of mushroom soup
1 cup chicken broth or milk
2 drops Tabasco
2 cans (6½ ounces each) tuna fish
1 tablespoon dried onion flakes, divided
¼ cup slivered almonds
1 bag (6½ ounces) potato chips, lightly crushed

Combine soup, broth, and Tabasco sauce. Place one can of tuna in a greased casserole dish. Sprinkle with half the onions and almonds; pour half the soup mixture over the top. Cover well with a layer of chips. Repeat process. Cover and bake at 300 degrees for 45 minutes; uncover and bake for another 15 minutes or until top layer of chips is crisp.

Yield: 4 to 6 servings

SEAFOOD ENCHILADAS

Sauce:

4 tablespoons butter
4 tablespoons flour
1 can chicken broth
1 cup milk
⅓ cup dry white wine
⅛ teaspoon cayenne pepper
1½ cups Monterey Jack cheese

Enchiladas:

1 pound imitation crab meat
½ pound fresh mushrooms, sliced
3 green onions, sliced
2 tablespoons butter
2 cups Monterey Jack cheese, shredded
Paprika
12 flour tortillas

In large glass bowl, microcook butter on high for 1 minute. Stir in flour and add liquids. Microcook on high 5 to 6 minutes, stirring every 2 minutes. Sauce should be thick and bubbly. Add cayenne pepper and cheese and stir until cheese is melted.

While sauce is cooking, sauté mushrooms and onion in butter. Add crab meat and cheese, stirring to mix well. Place ½ cup crab mixture in center of one flour tortilla. Roll tortilla and place, seam side down, in a greased oblong baking dish. Continue process with remaining tortillas. Pour ½ of sauce over enchiladas and bake 17 to 20 minutes at 350 degrees. To serve, ladle sauce over each enchilada and dust with paprika.

Yield: 12 servings

31

IRISH STEW

3 pounds lamb cubes or stew beef
1 can (28 ounces) tomatoes
1 box (20 ounces) frozen peas or green beans
6 whole carrots
3 medium potatoes, cubed
3 medium onions, chopped
1 cup chopped celery
3 tablespoons tapioca
1 tablespoon sugar
2 to 3 teaspoons salt
Dash black pepper
Pinch of thyme, marjoram, and rosemary
2 ounces red wine (optional)

Place all ingredients in a deep casserole dish or pan. Cover tightly and bake at 225 degrees for 5 hours. It is not necessary to brown the meat. Serve with dumplings (recipe follows).

Yield: 8 servings

DUMPLINGS

2 cups flour
4 teaspoons baking powder
Pinch of salt
1 egg, well beaten
1 cup milk (just enough for a stiff batter)
3 tablespoons butter, melted

Combine dry ingredients; stir in egg, milk, and butter. Drop batter, ¼ cup at a time, into hot stew. Cover and bake for ½ hour.

Yield: 8 servings

February

Cravings

Love laughs at obstacles, his arrow flies,
Now tipped with blushes, now with tender sighs.
. . . Oh love! Sweet love! from thy dear rosy shrine,
Wound one young heart and make it wholly mine.
And bless with peace thy constant Valentine!

Rock and Company, London

Valentines

The golden age of valentines was between 1840 and 1870. Most valentines in America at that time were still home-made. Love's messages were disguised with symbols. Every flower and every object had a special meaning. A white rose portrayed purity; a red rose, passionate love; yellow was for jealousy and lavender, mistrust. The honeysuckle represented devotion; peonies, anger. A bird cage indicated domestic intentions; a spider web, good luck; and a fish, fertility. Many times ink was scented with sweet-smelling lemon verbena, rosemary, lavender, or lily-of-the-valley. Gingerbread hearts were also a popular valentine during this time. The message of love touched all the senses as the valentine was gladly received.

Fun Tips

Chocolate-dipped fruit can be an alternative "Craving" to satisfy a sweet tooth. Melt your favorite chocolate bar and dip strawberries, cherries, grapes, or orange sections. Allow to dry at room temperature. Eat within 24 hours.

For a salty-sweet treat dip the bulb end of a cashew or a pretzel into melted white chocolate.

Sweet Hearts

Ham Loaf (p. 254)

Broccoli Rice Strata (p. 219)

Fluffy Pink Salad (p. 177)

Crusty French Bread (p. 79)

Lincoln Log Roll (p. 112) or

Cherry Cheesecake Tart (p. 132)

Pink Lady Cocktail (p. 195)

Peppermint Ice Cream Fudge (p. 40)

Valentines' Day

* ★ Bake cookies and take to a friend's house; leave on the doorstep, ring the bell and run.
* ★ Make old-fashioned valentines and send to friends.
* ★ Make happiness note jars or tree (hang a happy or loving thought for each day of the month or write something special you'll do for family members or friends)
* ★ Create festive placemats for valentines' dinner by weaving red and white construction paper. Decorate white paper napkins with holiday stickers to complete the table setting.

Presidents' Day

* ★ Fly the flag.
* ★ Read interesting stories about some of the Presidents.

Cravings

Candy

CHOCOLATE BAR DELIGHTS

3 bars (8 ounces each) Hershey Almond Chocolate
1 tub (12 ounces) frozen whipped topping
20 vanilla wafers, crushed

Melt chocolate. Add whipped topping and blend well. Chill 3 hours. Roll cold chocolate mixture into small balls; roll in crushed cookies. Freeze or refrigerate.

SUGAR COATED NUTS

1 cup sugar
½ teaspoon cinnamon
½ cup evaporated milk
½ teaspoon vanilla
2 cups pecans

Mix sugar and cinnamon; add milk. Bring to a boil and cook to soft ball stage. Add vanilla; pour over pecans. Separate nuts and cool.

PIONEER HONEY CANDY

2 cups honey
1 cup sugar
1 cup cream

Combine the ingredients and cook slowly until it reaches the hard ball stage. Pour onto a buttered platter. When cool enough to handle, butter hands and pull until a golden color. Cut in 1-inch pieces and wrap in waxed paper.

ROCKY ROAD FUDGE

1 cup miniature marshmallows
1 cup walnuts
1 cup sweetened condensed milk
1 cup semisweet chocolate chips
½ cup butter (1 square)

Melt butter in the microwave oven. Add chocolate chips and microcook one minute. Stir until smooth. Stir in milk. Fold in marshmallows and nuts; quickly pour into buttered oblong pan. Cool.

MICROWAVE PEANUT BRITTLE

1 cup sugar
½ cup corn syrup
1 cup raw peanuts
⅛ teaspoon salt
1 tablespoon butter
1 teaspoon soda
1 teaspoon vanilla

Combine sugar, corn syrup, peanuts, and salt in 8-cup microwave batter bowl. Microcook on high for 8 minutes, stirring once after 4 minutes. Add butter and microcook 1 minute or until mixture looks caramelized in color. Stir in soda and vanilla and pour out onto buttered cookie sheet.

CINNAMON MERINGUE NUTS

1 egg white
½ cup sugar
1 teaspoon cinnamon
Pinch of salt
2 cups whole pecans

Beat egg white until it stands in peaks. Fold in sugar, cinnamon, salt, and nuts. Drop onto a buttered baking sheet in clusters or singly. Bake at 300 degrees for 40 minutes.

Yield: ½ pound

SPICED WALNUTS

2 cups walnuts
1 teaspoon cinnamon
½ teaspoon cloves
¼ teaspoon allspice
1 cup sugar
3 tablespoons water

Combine sugar, water, and spices; mix well. Bring to a boil over medium heat, stirring. Add nuts and stir until nuts are glazed and toasted. Spread on baking sheet to cool, separate with fork.

Yield: 2 cups

PEPPERMINT ICE CREAM FUDGE

2 pounds dipping chocolate
1 pint vanilla ice cream
Peppermint flavoring to taste
¾ cup chopped pecans, optional

Break chocolate into chunks and melt in double boiler. Melt ice cream to a heavy sauce consistency. Place chocolate in a very large bowl and beat a few minutes, scraping bowl frequently. Gradually add ice cream, beating on medium-high speed, until mixture is thick and light brown (about 15 minutes). Add peppermint flavoring and nuts during last few minutes of beating time. Spread mixture in a buttered oblong pan. Refrigerate until mixture starts to get firm. Cut in small squares. Refrigerate until it is solid.

Stores several weeks in refrigerator. Don't freeze.

OLD-FASHIONED FUDGE

4½ cups sugar
1 can evaporated milk
¾ cup butter (1½ cubes)
2 bars (7 ounces each) plain Hershey Chocolate
1 package (12 ounces) chocolate chips
1 large jar marshmallow creme
2 cups chopped nuts

Bring sugar, milk, and butter to a rolling boil over medium heat and boil for 5 minutes. Pour over remaining ingredients in a large bowl. Beat until mixture begins to hold its shape. Pour into buttered oblong pan. Let set.

Variation: Add one package miniature marshmallows just before pouring into pan to set.

TASTY TAFFY

2 cups sugar
½ cup light corn syrup
¼ cup vinegar
¼ teaspoon cream of tartar
1 teaspoon vanilla
¼ cup water

Place sugar, corn syrup, water, vinegar, and cream of tartar in saucepan. Bring mixture to a boil, then lower the heat sufficiently to maintain a boil. Cook to hard crack stage (254 degrees for 4,500 feet altitude). Add vanilla. Pour onto buttered area. As soon as taffy is cooled enough to handle, add flavoring and bright food coloring. Pull taffy until candy becomes dull in color or too hard to pull. The sooner you can start to pull and the more air you incorporate, the better the taffy.

When the candy has been pulled to a dull color, pull candy into a long rope and twist. Then with a knife make indentations of desired candy size. When the candy hardens, it can be easily broken into pieces by striking the candy, which should break where indentations were made.

This colorful candy could be used to make a candy wreath to give away or welcome guests through the holiday season.

TOOTSIE ROLLS
(This is a fun recipe for children to help with)

2 tablespoons butter, softened
½ cup light corn syrup
2 squares unsweetened chocolate, melted
1 teaspoon vanilla
¾ cup instant powdered milk
3 cups powdered sugar

Blend butter, corn syrup, chocolate, and vanilla. Combine milk and sugar and stir into chocolate mixture.

Mixture will be crumbly so knead until well blended and smooth.

Roll into four long rolls. Either cut into individual pieces and wrap in waxed paper or wrap entire roll.

Best if kept refrigerated and served chilled.

Yield: 4 long rolls

ORANGE GLAZED PECANS

1½ cups sugar
½ cup orange juice
1 tablespoon grated orange peel
3 cups pecans

Combine sugar and orange juice in medium saucepan. Cook over medium heat, stirring constantly, until sugar is dissolved. Continue cooking without stirring until mixture reaches soft ball stage (238 degrees). Remove from heat. Add orange peel and pecans. Stir with a wooden spoon until mixture becomes creamy. Spoon onto waxed paper. Separate pecans with a fork. Let dry.

Yield: 1 pound

DIVINITY

2½ cups sugar
⅔ cup light corn syrup
2 egg whites, stiffly beaten
½ cup hot water
¼ teaspoon salt
½ teaspoon vanilla

Pour hot water over sugar, syrup, and salt in sauce pan, stir until sugar is dissolved. Cook without stirring until hard, almost brittle when tested in cold water. With damp cloth wash away any sugar crystals that may have formed on sides of saucepan. Remove from heat and pour gradually over egg whites. Beat mixture constantly, using wire whisk, until divinity holds its shape when dropped from spoon. Add vanilla and drop candy by spoonfuls onto greased paper or pour into greased pan and cut into squares.

Variations: 1 cup nut meats, candied cherries, or browned coconut may be added when mixture is ready to drop. Pastel tints of green, pink, yellow, or lavender in divinity are attractive.

Note: Beat egg whites as the syrup finishes cooking.

SPUN PINK-CINNAMON POPCORN

2 quarts popped popcorn
¾ cup sugar
¼ cup light corn syrup
3 tablespoons water
1 tablespoon red cinnamon candy

Place popped corn in large buttered bowl. Combine remaining ingredients in small saucepan. Heat slowly, stirring constantly, to boiling point. Cook without stirring to 272 degrees—soft crack stage. Remove from heat and drizzle over popcorn, stirring to coat. When well-mixed, pour onto buttered cookie sheet and bake at 325 degrees for about 10 minutes. Separate kernels when cool.

Yield: 2 quarts

March

Soup, Sippets, and Sandwiches

The year's at the Spring
And day's at the Morn
God's in his Heaven
All's right with the World.

Robert Browning

Sippet

A sippet is a small piece of bread that is dipped in soup. They can be made by using triangles of pita bread, lightly buttered, sprinkled with freshly grated Parmesan cheese or herbs and broiled until crisp. Store in an airtight container. A basket of sippets adds a special flair to a warm soup dinner.

Fun Tips

Toppings on soup can add interest and flavor. Some suggestions are: popcorn, croutons, dollop of sour cream, thin lemon slice, sniped chives or parsley, or grated cheese.

A squeeze of lemon in hot or cold soups intensifies the flavor.

Serve soup in a large hollowed-out french bread bun.

To make sandwiches fun for children to eat, cut out each slice of bread with a cookie cutter before making the sandwich. For adults use two different kinds of bread when making sandwiches.

Feast of St. Patrick

Irish Stew and Dumplings (p. 32)

Irish Soda Bread (p. 84)

Spinach Salad (p. 159) or Lime Salad (p. 175)

Grasshopper Sundae (p. 111)

Cookie

Mock Mint Julep (p. 201)

St. Patrick's Day Party

* Men wear green arm bands.
* Women wear a green bow on dress or blouse.
* Tint water for ice cubes green.
* Use leprechauns and green and white carnations for centerpiece.
* Play Irish music during dinner (can be checked out from library)
* Read a story about leprechauns.

Other

* Have a kite flying day.
* Make pinwheels with construction paper and a drinking straw.
* Plan a family "Academy Award" Night. Spotlight each member of the family and tell about the most outstanding achievement they have accomplished for the past year or why they are a special part of the family. Present a small trophy or ribbon to each person.
* When pruning fruit trees, save a nicely shaped branch with lots of twigs. Secure the branch in a pot filled with sand and use it all year as a holiday "tree." Hang ornaments and tie the branches with multicolored bows to fit the season.

Soup, Sippets, and Sandwiches

TURKEY SOUP

8 cups chicken broth
1 cup cubed potato
1 cup sliced carrots
1 cup sliced celery
¼ cup chopped onion
1 package (10 ounces) frozen baby lima beans, optional
1 cup uncooked noodles
2 cups diced cooked turkey
1 teaspoon salt

Cook raw vegetables in chicken broth for 10 minutes. Add lima beans and noodles and continue cooking until vegetables and noodles are tender. Add turkey and season with salt. Heat thoroughly.

TURKEY CORN CHOWDER

1 cup thinly sliced onion
¼ cup butter
2 cups diced (about ¼ inch) potatoes
1 cup thinly sliced celery
1 cup water
2 teaspoons salt
1 chicken bouillon cube
3 cups milk
3 cups diced cooked turkey or chicken
1 can (1 pound 1 ounce) cream-style corn
½ teaspoon thyme
¼ cup chopped parsley

In large Dutch oven or saucepan sauté onion slowly in butter until tender, but not brown. Add potatoes, celery, water, salt, and bouillon cube. Cover and cook until potatoes and celery are tender, about 15 minutes. Add milk, turkey or chicken, corn, and thyme. Heat to serving temperature. Just before serving, stir in parsley.

Yield: 8 to 10 servings

WILD RICE SOUP

6 tablespoons margarine or butter
1 tablespoon minced onion
½ cup flour
3 cups chicken broth
2 cups cooked wild rice
⅓ cup minced ham
½ cup finely grated carrots
3 tablespoons chopped slivered almonds
½ teaspoon salt
1 cup half and half
Minced parsley or chives

Melt margarine in saucepan; sauté onion until tender. Blend in flour; gradually add broth. Cook, stirring constantly, until mixture comes to a boil; boil 1 minute. Stir in rice, ham, carrots, almonds, and salt; simmer about 5 minutes. Blend in half and half, heat to serving temperature. Garnish with minced parsley or chives.

LOW-CAL VEGGIE SOUP

5 cups tomato juice
3 cups water
½ cabbage, chopped
2 cans (4 ounces each) drained mushrooms
1 onion, chopped
½ teaspoon garlic powder
1 bay leaf
½ teaspoon Mr. Dash
3 zucchini (chopped)
1 can green beans (French style) including juice
3 ribs celery, chopped
5 beef bouillon cubes

Combine all ingredients and simmer one hour. Sprinkle crisp bacon pieces over top, if desired.

MARTI'S BORSCHT

> 1 can (16 ounces) diced beets
> 1 can (14½ ounces) beef consommé
> 1 carton (8 ounces) cottage cheese
> ½ cup sour cream
> 1 teaspoon sugar
> 1 lemon, juiced
> 1 tablespoon minced onion
> 3 teaspoons Worcestershire sauce

Combine all ingredients in a blender container and puree. Chill. Serve cold and garnish with dollop of sour cream.

Yield: 8 servings

COLD LEMON SOUP

> 1 can (10¾ ounces) tomato soup
> 3 cups buttermilk
> Lemon zest
>   OR finely grated lemon rind

Combine all ingredients in a blender container and blend well. Chill. Serve cold and garnish with lemon zest and sprig of mint.

Yield: 8 servings

GAZPACHO SOUP

1 can (46 ounces) tomato juice
1 bottle (12 ounces) seafood cocktail sauce
½ cup sugar (scant)
2 cups chopped celery
1 tablespoon minced onion
     OR 1 small onion, chopped
½ cup chopped green pepper
1½ teaspoons horseradish
2 tablespoons lemon juice
1 tablespoon Worcestershire sauce
¼ teaspoon garlic salt
2 cans broken shrimp
Salt to taste

Mix all ingredients together and chill overnight.

Yield: 10 servings

SPLIT PEA SOUP

2 quarts water
2 cups green split peas
1 rib celery, diced
1 large carrot, diced
1 small onion, chopped
¼ teaspoon thyme
1 pinch cayenne pepper
1 bay leaf
Salt and pepper

Combine all ingredients and boil vigorously for 20 minutes. Continue cooking slowly until the peas are done. Strain this mixture through a colander. If soup is too thick, thin with a little water. Season to taste.
Note: Recipe can be doubled.

Yield: 8 servings

CREAM OF ZUCCHINI SOUP

½ pound (2 medium) onions, chopped
2 tablespoons butter
1½ pounds zucchini squash, sliced
3 cups chicken broth
⅛ teaspoon black pepper
⅛ teaspoon nutmeg
⅛ teaspoon salt
Pinch cayenne pepper
½ cup half and half
Grated Cheddar cheese

Sauté onions in butter until tender. Combine onions, zucchini, and chicken broth in heavy saucepan; bring to a boil, simmer 15 minutes. Add seasonings and put mixture in blender container. Puree until smooth. Add half and half. Season to taste. Reheat—don't boil. Garnish with cheese.

Yield: 8 servings

SENATE BEAN SOUP

1½ cups dry great Northern beans
1 smoked ham hock
1 medium potato, finely diced
1 onion, diced
½ cup diced celery
1 clove garlic, minced
Salt and pepper
Chopped parsley

Soak beans overnight in 1 quart water. For quick soak, bring beans and water to boil and boil 2 minutes. Cover and let stand 1 hour. Drain beans and measure liquid. Add enough water to make 2 quarts. Place soaked beans, water, and ham hock in kettle. Cover and simmer 2 hours. Add potato, onion, celery, and garlic. Simmer 1 hour. Remove ham hock and cut up meat. Remove 1 cup beans, potatoes, and some liquid. Puree in blender. Use this as a thickener for soup. Return meat and pureed beans to soup. Heat. Season to taste with salt and pepper. Sprinkle with chopped parsley.

Yield: 6 servings

AUNTIE'S OYSTER STEW

2 cans (8 ounces each) whole oysters, drained,
    reserving juice
1 tablespoon butter
2 tablespoons crushed salted crackers
1 quart milk or half and half
Salt and pepper
Paprika for garnish

Place oysters in strainer and run cold water over them.
Place oysters back in oyster juice. Melt butter in pan, add
cracker crumbs and mix well. Add milk, oysters, and the juice.
Simmer until oysters curl, season to taste. Garnish with paprika.

FROSTY STRAWBERRY SOUP

3 pints strawberries
½ cup sugar
¼ cup honey
2 quarts whipping cream
1 tablespoon lemon juice
¼ cup sherry (optional)

Puree strawberries, sugar, and honey. Combine remaining ingredients and chill. Delicious.

MEXICAN BUFFET SOUP

2 tablespoons butter
1 tablespoon olive oil
2 cups chopped onions
2 tablespoons flour
1 can (28 ounces) tomatoes (pureed)
4 cans (14½ ounces each) beef broth
1 clove garlic, minced
1 tablespoon wine vinegar
1 tablespoon Worcestershire sauce
½ teaspoon pepper
½ teaspoon oregano
¼ teaspoon tarragon
¼ teaspoon cumin

Sauté onion in butter and olive oil. Add flour and mix well. Add remaining ingredients and bring to a boil.

Prepare small bowls of:
    ham cubes
    chopped hard boiled eggs
    hamburger balls, cooked
    cooked chopped onions or chives
    shrimp
    chopped olives
    garbanzo beans
    celery
    broccoli
    carrots, parboiled

Instruct guests to fill their soup bowls with desired meats and vegetables. Pour hot boiling broth over mixture.

Note: Each guest could bring a bowl of meat or vegetables.

TACO SOUP

1 pound lean ground beef

¾ cup chopped onion

2 cans (16 ounces each) stewed tomatoes

2 cans (16 ounces each) kidney beans with liquid

1 can (16 ounces) tomato sauce

3 cups water

4 teaspoons taco seasoning mix

Toppings:

sour cream

grated cheese

diced green onions

guacamole (optional)

broken tortilla chips

Brown beef and onion. Add remaining ingredients and simmer for 2 hours. Serve with toppings.

HAM AND CHEESE SOUP

4 cups diced potatoes
1 cup sliced celery
1 cup diced carrots
½ cup diced onions
3 cups water
½ cup margarine or butter
½ cup flour
4 cups milk
2 teaspoons salt
Pepper to taste
1 pound cheddar cheese, grated
2 cups cooked ham.

Cook vegetables in water until tender. Melt margarine or butter and add flour, mixing well. Slowly add milk and seasonings and bring to a boil. Add cream sauce to undrained vegetables. Add cheese and ham and heat thoroughly.

POTATO SOUP

3 slices bacon, cooked and cut to bite size pieces
    (reserve grease)
⅓ cup chopped onions
2 cups diced potatoes
½ cup diced celery
¾ cup canned milk
¼ cup flour
Dash pepper
1 tablespoon parsley
½ teaspoon basil
¼ teaspoon onion salt
¼ teaspoon garlic salt
½ teaspoon celery salt

Sauté onion in a little bacon grease until tender. Add vegetables. Cover with water. Cook for 5 minutes or until tender. Add enough water to make 2 cups. Combine remaining ingredients, mixing well, and add to undrained vegetables. Simmer for 5 minutes. Add cooked bacon and serve.

Yield: 6 servings

EASY SEAFOOD CHOWDER

1 can minced clams, broken shrimp, or crab, drained
1 can (10¾ ounces) cream of mushroom soup
1 can (10¾ ounces) cream of celery soup
1 can (10¾ ounces) tomato soup
1½ cups half and half
2½ cups milk

Combine all ingredients and heat.

Yield: 6 servings

PRONTO CHILI

1 can (30 ounces) chili with meat and beans
1 can (15½ ounces) kidney beans
1 can (15½ ounces) pork and beans
2 cans (8 ounces each) tomato sauce
1 onion, chopped
1 green pepper, chopped (optional)
1 pound ground beef
2 tablespoons packaged chili seasonings
Grated cheese for garnish

Brown meat, onion, and pepper. Drain fat, if necessary. Add canned ingredients and chili seasoning and simmer for 30 minutes. Serve hot, garnish with grated cheese.

Yield: 6 to 8 servings

OLD FASHIONED VEGETABLE SOUP

1 pound shortribs
Stew meat, as desired
Celery salt
Onion salt
Garlic salt
Shortening or oil for browning meat
4 cups water
1 carrot, sliced
1 whole onion
Handful of celery leaves
Carrots as desired, sliced
Potatoes as desired, diced
Celery as desired, sliced
2 cans (18¾ ounces each) tomatoes, chopped
1 can stewed tomatoes
1 can pearl onions and juice
¼ cup capers, drained
Dash thyme
Dash marjoram
Dash rosemary
Dash paprika

Season meat with celery salt, onion salt, and garlic salt. Melt shortening in an electric frying pan at a low temperature; add ribs and stew meat. Brown meat, (long, lazy browning for 1 hour). Add water, 1 carrot, whole onion, and celery leaves; simmer 4 hours adding water as needed. Remove meat and strain broth. Set aside. Parboil carrots, potatoes, and celery. Add tomatoes, pearl onions and juice, capers, broth, and seasonings. Simmer 1 hour to blend flavors.

CHILLED RASPBERRY SOUP

2 cups fresh raspberries
    OR 2 packages (10 ounces each) frozen raspberries
½ cup water
1 cup cranberry juice
1 tablespoon lemon juice
2 cartons (8 ounces each) raspberry yogurt
⅓ cup whipped cream
Cinnamon

Combine raspberries and water in blender and puree until smooth. Add cranberry juice and lemon juice. Strain soup into large bowl. Add yogurt and whisk until well blended. Cover; refrigerate until cold. Garnish each serving with whipped cream; sprinkle with cinnamon.

Yield: 6 servings

CHILI

2 pounds ground beef
3 large onions, chopped
2 large green peppers, chopped
3 scant cups small red chili beans, soaked overnight and
   cooked until tender
   OR 2 cans kidney beans
1 can (28 ounces) tomatoes, diced
1 can (10¾ ounces) cream of tomato soup
1 can (46 ounces) tomato juice
1½ teaspoons salt
¼ teaspoon paprika
¼ teaspoon cayenne pepper
5 whole cloves
2 bay leaves
4 tablespoons chili powder

Brown ground beef; add onion and cook until tender. Combine all ingredients in a large kettle and simmer for 1 or more hours.

CREAMY MUSHROOM SOUP

½ cup butter
1½ cups chopped green onions, including tops
4 cups chopped fresh mushrooms
4 tablespoons flour
2 cups half and half
2 cups chicken broth
½ teaspoon salt
¼ teaspoon pepper

Sauté green onions in butter over low heat until tender. Add chopped mushrooms and cook, stirring, for 2 minutes. Stir in flour and continue cooking and stirring for 3 minutes. Remove from heat and pour chicken broth and half and half in a steady stream, stirring gently. Bring to a boil over moderate heat. Simmer, stirring, for 5 minutes. Season to taste.

Yield: 8 servings

DOUBLE DUTY SANDWICHES OR SALAD

1 can (6½ ounces) tuna
1 cup chopped celery
3 hard-boiled eggs, chopped
2 pimentos, chopped
1 teaspoon salt
⅛ teaspoon pepper
2 tablespoons chopped dill pickles
2 tablespoons finely chopped onion
2 tablespoons lemon juice
¾ cup mayonnaise

Drain tuna and break into chunks. Combine with rest of ingredients. Serve on crisp greens, or use to stuff tomatoes or small avocado halves for salad. Or spread on bread, allowing ⅓ to ½ cup for each sandwich.

Yield: 10 to 12 sandwiches or 4 to 6 salads

STUFFED FRENCH ROLLS

1 pound cheese, grated
1 can (4 ounces) ripe olives
1 can (4 ounces) green chilis
4 hard boiled eggs, sliced
Salt to taste
½ cup oil
1 large onion, chopped
3 dozen French rolls

In a blender container, combine all ingredients except rolls and blend. Fill French rolls with cheese mixture and wrap each roll in foil; put in a paper bag. Bake at 250 degrees for 45 minutes.

MONSTER CLAW SANDWICHES

1 can (11 ounces) refrigerated soft breadsticks
2 tablespoons margarine, melted
8 thin square slices cooked ham, cut diagonally
8 slices American cheese, cut diagonally in half
16 toothpicks

Heat oven to 350 degrees. Unroll dough; separate at per-forations to form 8 strips. Cut each strip in half crosswise, form-ing 16 smaller strips. Place 1 inch apart on ungreased cookie sheets. Make two 1½ inch cuts in one end of each strip. To form claws, spread cut sections of each strip apart. Bake for 11 to 16 minutes or until golden brown. Brush claws with margarine. Remove from cookie sheet; cool completely. Wrap 1 ham triangle and 1 cheese triangle around center of each breadstick, leaving claw uncovered. Secure with toothpick.

BARBECUE BURGER MIX

    1 pound ground beef
    ½ cup chopped onion
    ¼ cup chopped green pepper
    ¼ cup chopped celery
    1 can (8 ounces) tomato sauce
    ¼ cup catsup
    1 tablespoon vinegar
    1½ teaspoons Worcestershire sauce
    ⅛ teaspoon pepper
    6 hamburger buns

Brown meat, add vegetables. Cook until vegetables are tender. Add remaining ingredients; mix well. Cover. Simmer 20 minutes. Spoon on hamburger buns.

Yield: 6 servings

GRILLED TOMATO & CHEESE SANDWICH

    4 diagonal slices Italian bread (½ inch thick)
    1 teaspoon spicy brown mustard
    1 small tomato, cut into 4 slices
    2 ounces shredded Monterey Jack cheese
    ¼ cup prepared guacamole
    ⅓ cup alfalfa sprouts

Spread bread with mustard. Top each with tomato slice and cheese. Broil just until cheese is melted, about 2 minutes. Top with guacamole and alfalfa sprouts. Broil for 2 minutes.

Yield: 4 servings

CHEESE SANDWICH

½ pound Colby cheese, grated
2 green onions, thinly sliced
1 tablespoon finely diced green pepper
Salad dressing or mayonnaise
4 hamburger buns

Combine cheese, onions, and green pepper. Mix with enough salad dressing or mayonnaise until moist, spread on hamburger buns. Broil just until cheese melts.

CRAB SANDWICHES

2 to 3 English muffins or buns
1 can crab meat
½ can cream of tomato soup
2 tablespoons butter
1 tablespoon Worcestershire sauce
½ green pepper, chopped
Small bottle green stuffed olives, sliced
½ pound American cheese, grated
Garlic salt to taste

Slice buns or English muffins. Combine rest of ingredients and blend well. Place mixture on bun halves and bake at 350 degrees for 20 minutes.

Taco Pocket

5 Pita bread
1 package (¼ ounce) taco seasoning mix
1 pound ground beef
1 carton (8 ounces) sour cream
¼ head lettuce, chopped
¼ pound cheddar cheese, grated
2 tomatoes, chopped
1 avocado, chopped

Fry ground beef. Drain. Mix in seasoning according to directions on package. Slice bread crosswise; spread both sides of the pocket with sour cream. Layer the ingredients, starting at one side of the pocket and building to the other side.

Yield: 10 half sandwiches

STROGANOFF SANDWICH

1 loaf French bread
1½ pounds ground beef
4 tablespoons onion, chopped
1½ cups Cheddar cheese, grated
½ cup sour cream
1 can (10¾ ounces) cream of mushroom soup
1 tablespoon Worcestershire sauce
Salt and pepper
2 tomatoes, chopped
1 green pepper, chopped

Slice bread lengthwise. Lightly spread butter and wrap in foil. Bake at 350 degrees for 15 minutes.

Brown meat. Drain. Add onion and cook until transparent. Remove from heat, add sour cream, Worcestershire sauce, salt, and pepper. Remove bread from oven. Spread meat mixture on each half. Arrange tomatoes and green pepper on top. Sprinkle with cheese. Place back in oven to melt cheese.

Yield: 6 to 8 servings

LUNCH BOX POINTERS

1. Sandwiches are the main attraction of the lunch box, so to avoid monotony, vary breads and use egg, fish, cheese, meat, poultry, peanut butter fillings.

2. Place sandwiches in sandwich bags to keep them fresh and avoid mingling of flavors.

3. Plan ahead; freeze sandwiches to save time in morning. Especially good idea in warm weather.

4. Place crisp vegetables, lettuce, olives, pickles, and cheese cubes in sandwich bags.

5. Put salads in plastic containers.

6. Put fruit in every box; varieties of fresh, dried, or small cans.

7. Include thermos of soups.

8. Add deviled egg or hard-boiled egg in plastic bag.

9. Include packaged cookies, cup cakes, cheese crackers, dried fruits, marshmallows, popcorn balls, salted nuts, and semisweet chocolate pieces.

10. Include paper napkins, paper cups, and when necessary, plastic spoons and forks.

April

A Slice of Spring

In spring a young man's fancy
lightly turns to thoughts of love.

Alfred Lord Tennyson

A good laugh is sunshine in the house.

William Makepeace Thackeray

Centerpieces

Centerpieces add flair, interest, beauty, and perhaps whimsy to your table setting. Purchased flower arrangements, although always beautiful, can be expensive to use often. Use your imagination and create individualized arrangements. Remember, keep them lower or higher than eye level or remove them before guests are seated. Some ideas to get you started:

* Branches of willows, cherry, or apple blossoms in a clear glass vase or pitcher lined with colored tissue paper.
* Baskets of fresh herbs, fruits, or vegetables.
* One flower set by every place.

* Sea shells.
* Tiny potted green plants wrapped in colored foil.
* Small clay pots planted with flowering plants.
* Several small brown lunch sacks, tops rolled down, filled with nuts, dried fruit, or goodies.
* Bosc pears, Granny Smith apples, and fresh ivy set among white pillar candles.
* Grapevine wreath filled with fat pillar candles of varying heights.
* A traditional Williamsburg style S-swag of evergreens or boxwood accented with a large pineapple and fresh fruit.
* Hang streamers of ribbons from the light fixture over the table.
* Use heirlooms such as teapots, teacups, egg cups, etc., and explain the sentimental value to family and friends.

Fun Tips

Spring violets are a symbol of humility and modesty. They can be eaten in salads, floated in punch, or crystallized and used as pastry decorations.

Sprinkle chocolate chips into waffle, pancake or quick bread batter, or sprinkle chopped pecans into pancake batter and top cooked pancakes with cinnamon and sugar and warm maple syrup.

Top pancakes with warm apple pie filling.

Make butter molds, curls, or balls for serving with your special breads.

Make french toast with day-old croissants, flavored with ground cinnamon, grated orange zest, and vanilla.

Bread can be baked in a variety of containers for a festive appearance. Use cans, molds, or clean clay pots.

Easter Dinner

Company Ham (p. 253)

Lemon Cashew Asparagus (p. 218)

Potato Casserole (p. 218)

Surprise Salad (p. 176)

Refrigerator Rolls (p. 81)

Strawberry Angel Torte (p. 114) or

Lemon Charlotte (p. 133)

Blushing Lemonade (p. 196)

Easter

* ★ Grow your own Easter grass by sprouting wheat.
* ★ Make an Easter egg cake and hide coins wrapped in foil inside the cake. Set cake on bed of green coconut.
* ★ Place small coins in plastic eggs to hide. Give a prize to the one who found the most money. This could be a pair of stockings with a check inside for savings "socked away."
* ★ Color Easter eggs with: markers, crayons, stickers, or dye. Give a prize to the wildest, prettiest, most creative, etc.
* ★ Decorate marshmallow cupcakes as bunnies using licorice strings, tiny jelly beans, pink paper for the bunny ears, and red cinnamon candies.
* ★ Organize an Easter Parade—supply a creative box of supplies and let everyone make a hat.

★ Tell the story of the resurrection—each person sharing one event.

April Fools

★ Have a backward party—everyone dress backwards, say good-bye instead of hello, serve dessert first, etc.

A Slice of Spring

Breads

CRUSTY FRENCH BREAD

2 packages dry yeast
½ cup warm water
2 cups hot water
3 tablespoons sugar
1 tablespoon salt
5 tablespoons shortening, melted, or vegetable oil
6 cups flour, unsifted
1 egg white
Sesame seeds

Dissolve yeast in ½ cup warm water. Let stand 10 minutes. In large bowl combine 2 cups hot water, sugar, salt, shortening, and half of the flour; beat well. Stir in dissolved yeast. Stir in remaining flour. Mix well. Leaving spoon in batter, allow to rest again for 10 more minutes. Repeat 3 more times. Turn out dough onto floured board. Knead once or twice until lightly coated with flour. Divide dough in half. Roll each half into a 9x12-inch rectangle. Starting at long edge, roll loosely as for jelly roll. Seal edge. Place both rolls seam side down, on one large baking sheet. Slash top of each loaf diagonally 3 times with a sharp knife. Brush with beaten egg white. Sprinkle with sesame seeds. Let rise 30 minutes more. Bake at 400 degrees for 35 minutes (until golden brown).

Yield: 2 loaves

OUT OF THIS WORLD ROLLS

2 packages (2 tablespoons) active dry yeast
¼ cup warm water
½ cup shortening
    OR ½ cup margarine or butter, softened
½ cup sugar
3 eggs, well beaten
1 cup warm water
2 teaspoons salt
4½ cups flour

Soften yeast in the ¼ cup warm water. In large bowl, combine shortening (or margarine or butter), sugar, beaten eggs, 1 cup warm water, and salt. Stir in softened yeast and 2½ cups flour. Beat with hand mixer until smooth and well blended.

Add remaining flour, mixing with hands, to make soft dough; mix well. Cover and allow to rise in warm place until doubled in bulk, about one hour. Punch dough down and place in refrigerator overnight.

Three hours before baking, roll out by dividing dough in two portions. Roll each portion on lightly floured surface to rectangle ½ inch thick. Spread with softened butter. Roll jelly-roll style and cut in 1-inch slices.

Place slices cut-side down in greased muffin cups. Cover and allow to rise three hours. Bake at 400 degrees for 12 to 15 minutes, until lightly browned.

Yield: 24 large dinner rolls

Variation: Make a paste of orange juice, butter, and sugar. Spread on dough before rolling jelly-roll style and cut in 1-inch slices by looping thread around the dough and pulling tight to cut. Bake as directed.

REFRIGERATOR ROLLS

½ cup mashed potatoes
½ cup lard
⅓ cup sugar
2 cups scalded milk
1 tablespoon yeast
½ cup warm water
2 cups flour
1 teaspoon salt
1 teaspoon baking powder
½ teaspoon soda

Dissolve yeast in warm water. Mix potatoes, lard, and sugar together. Add scalded milk; cool until tepid. Add yeast and dry ingredients and beat thoroughly. Add enough more flour to make a dough and knead thoroughly. Grease top of dough; cover, and place in refrigerator overnight. Shape and place in pans about 2 hours before baking. Bake at 400 degrees for 12 to 15 minutes.

Dough may be stored in refrigerator 4 to 5 days before using.

STICKY CARAMEL ROLLS

1½ cups pecan pieces
1 cup brown sugar
1 package (3⅝ ounces) instant butterscotch pudding mix
1 cup butter, melted
20 frozen dinner rolls

Spread pecans on bottom of rectangular pan. Combine brown sugar and pudding mix; sprinkle over pecans. Pour butter over sugar mixture and place rolls on top. Refrigerate overnight. Let rolls rise. Bake at 375 degrees for 20 to 25 minutes. Turn out onto foil or a serving platter.

Yield: 20 rolls

MALTED BREAD STICKS

1 ½ cups warm water
1 tablespoon honey
1 package yeast
3 to 4 cups flour
1 tablespoon malted milk powder
1 teaspoon salt
½ cup melted butter
Seasoning salt
Parmesan cheese
Sesame seeds

Combine water, honey, and yeast. Mix malted milk powder, salt, and enough flour to yeast mixture to form a soft, sticky dough. Knead 5 minutes. Roll out dough and cut into sticks. Brush with melted butter and sprinkle with seasoning salt, Parmesan cheese, or sesame seeds. Bake at 400 degrees for 15 minutes.

Yield: 2 to 3 dozen sticks

APRICOT TWISTS

1 cup sour cream
2 tablespoons shortening
3 tablespoons sugar
1 teaspoon salt
1 egg, beaten
1 tablespoon yeast
2½ cups flour
1 package (8 ounces) cream cheese, softened
¾ cup apricot jam
1 cup shredded coconut
½ cup chopped walnuts or pecans
½ cup apricot jam

Combine sour cream, shortening, sugar, salt, egg, yeast, and flour to make a stiff dough. Turn onto a lightly floured board and knead 2 minutes or until elastic and smooth. Set aside for 15 minutes.

Roll dough into an 18x10-inch rectangle. Spread with cream cheese, then ¾ cup apricot jam. Sprinkle with coconut and nuts. Fold rectangle into thirds lengthwise. Using a sharp knife or string, cut dough crosswise into 1-inch strips. Holding strips at each end, twist in opposite directions. Place twists on well-greased baking sheet. Bake at 375 degrees for 20 to 25 minutes or until golden brown.

In small saucepan, heat ½ cup apricot jam until soft enough to brush over twists. Remove baked twists from baking sheet and cool on a rack. While still warm, brush with warmed jam and sprinkle with coconut.

Yield: 18 twists

CHEESY BREAD ROLL

1 teaspoon garlic salt
1 cup scallions
2 cups grated cheese
1 loaf frozen bread dough (Rhodes), thawed
2 tablespoons butter, melted

Mix garlic salt, scallions, and cheese. Roll out bread dough; spread with cheese mixture and roll up jelly-roll fashion. Place dough in a bread pan; snip top 3 times and brush with melted butter. Let rise and bake according to package instructions.

IRISH SODA BREAD

4 cups flour
3 tablespoons sugar
½ teaspoon salt
1 teaspoon baking soda
2 teaspoons cream of tartar
1 cup raisins
2 eggs, beaten
1½ cups buttermilk

Sift flour, sugar, salt, soda, and cream of tartar into mixing bowl. Add raisins. Combine eggs and buttermilk; add to flour mixture, blending well. Knead a few minutes lightly. Form into round loaf; place on floured cookie sheet or pizza pan. Bake at 350 degrees for 45 minutes.

ZUCCHINI BREAD

3 cups flour
2 cups sugar
1 teaspoon salt
1 teaspoon soda
¼ teaspoon baking powder
1 teaspoon cinnamon
½ teaspoon ginger
½ teaspoon ground cloves
1 cup oil
3 eggs, beaten
2 cups grated zucchini
1 tablespoon vanilla
Nuts (optional)

Combine all dry ingredients and stir to mix. Make a well in the center of the dry ingredients and add all the remaining ingredients. Stir gently until blended.

Pour into 2 large loaf pans and bake at 350 degrees for 1 hour.

Yield: 2 large loaves

Banana Bread

1 cup sugar
½ cup shortening
1½ cups flour
1 teaspoon soda
1 teaspoon baking powder
1 teaspoon salt
2 eggs
3 or 4 bananas, mashed
¾ cup nuts
1 teaspoon vanilla

Cream sugar and shortening. Sift dry ingredients together and add to sugar and shortening mixture. Add eggs and vanilla. Fold in bananas and nuts.

Bake in wax paper-lined loaf pans at 350 degrees for 45 minutes.

Yield: two small loaves.

Note: This recipe can be baked in 1 large loaf pan for 55 minutes.

BANANA NUT COFFEE CAKE

1⅔ cups sugar
⅔ cup shortening
3 eggs
1 teaspoon vanilla
3½ cups flour
½ cup nonfat dry milk
2½ teaspoons baking powder
1 teaspoon baking soda
¼ teaspoon salt
½ cup water
1½ cups mashed ripe bananas
1 cup chopped walnuts

Cream sugar and shortening in large mixing bowl. Beat in eggs one at a time. Add vanilla. Combine flour, dry nonfat milk, baking powder, baking soda, and salt; blend into creamed mixture alternately with water. Stir in banana and nuts. Spoon into buttered 10-inch tube pan. Bake in slow oven (325 degrees) about 50 to 60 minutes or until toothpick comes out clean.

Yield: 1 coffee cake

SEVEN-WEEK BRAN MUFFINS

4 cups All-Bran cereal
2 cups 40% Bran Flakes
1 cup chopped dates
2 cups boiling water
1 cup shortening
2 cups sugar
4 eggs
1 quart buttermilk
5 cups flour
4 teaspoons soda
1 teaspoon salt
1 cup chopped nuts

Mix cereals, dates, and water; cool. Cream shortening and sugar and add remaining ingredients and cereal mixture.

Bake at 400 degrees for 20 minutes.

Note: Batter may be stored in refrigerator for as long as 7 weeks, or bake entire recipe and freeze.

WHOLE WHEAT CHEESE MUFFINS

1 cup flour
1 cup whole wheat flour
1 tablespoon baking powder
¾ teaspoon salt
3 tablespoons sugar
1 cup grated cheddar cheese
Dash of paprika
1 egg, well beaten
1 cup milk
3 tablespoons melted shortening

Mix all dry ingredients, cheese, and paprika. Combine egg, milk, and shortening and add to flour mixture, stirring only until flour disappears.

Fill greased muffin tins ⅔ full and bake at 425 degrees for 20 to 30 minutes.

DUTCH APPLE MUFFINS

1 package (18 ounces) spice cake mix
1½ cups fruit, nut and oat cereal (granola type)
1 cup chopped dates or raisins
1 cup chopped nuts
½ teaspoon ground cinnamon
¼ teaspoon ground nutmeg
1½ cups applesauce
4 eggs, well beaten
½ cup oil

In a medium bowl, combine dry cake mix, cereal, dates, nuts, and spices. Stir to distribute evenly. Add applesauce, beaten eggs, and oil. Fold gently until dry ingredients are moistened. Do not over-mix. Spoon into paper-lined muffin cups.

Topping:
1½ cups fruit, nut and oat cereal (granola type)
½ cup butter, melted
½ cup brown sugar
½ cup flour

Mix well. Spoon 1 tablespoon on each filled muffin cup. Bake at 350 degrees.

Yield: 24 muffins

BISCUITS AND GRAVY
BAKING POWDER BISCUITS

2 cups flour
4 teaspoons baking powder
½ teaspoon salt
¼ cup shortening
¾ cup milk

Sift dry ingredients into mixing bowl. Cut in fat until mixture has consistency of course cornmeal. Pour milk all at once into fat–flour mixture and stir vigorously until it thickens to the point where it will follow the spoon around the bowl.

Turn dough onto lightly floured board and without delay knead vigorously for about twenty seconds. Form dough into ball, then pat it with hand or roll to desired thickness and cut with floured biscuit cutter.

Bake at 425 degrees for 12 to 15 minutes.

Yield: 10 biscuits.

Variations on Biscuits

Pinwheel Biscuits: Roll dough ½ inch thick; spread with melted butter and sprinkle with sugar and cinnamon. Roll and cut in ½ inch slices. Bake, cut side down, on greased baking sheet in hot oven (450 degrees) 12 to 15 minutes.

Butterscotch Biscuits: Roll dough ½ inch thick. Spread with melted butter; sprinkle with brown sugar and chopped nut meats. Roll and cut in ½-inch slices. Bake, cut side down, on greased baking sheet in hot oven (450 degrees) 12 to 15 minutes.

Orange Biscuits: Add grated rind of 1 orange to biscuit

recipe. Arrange biscuits on greased baking sheet. Dip cube of sugar quickly into orange juice and press gently into center of each biscuit. Bake in hot oven (450 degrees) 12 to 15 minutes.

Cheese Swirls: Roll dough ½ inch thick; cover with grated American cheese and finely chopped pimento, if desired. Roll and cut in ½-inch slices. Bake, cut side down, on greased baking sheet in moderately hot oven (425 degrees) 15 minutes.

Jelly Triangles: Make biscuit dough with 2 tablespoons additional shortening. Roll ¼ inch thick and cut in 3-inch squares. On each square place a teaspoon of tart jelly; fold square diagonally and press edges together. Bake on ungreased baking sheet in hot oven (450 degrees) 12 to 15 minutes.

Drop Biscuits: Increase milk to 1 cup and drop from teaspoon on ungreased baking sheet. Bake in hot oven (450 degrees) 12 to 15 minutes. This makes a very crusty biscuit.

Whole-Wheat Biscuits: Substitute 1 cup whole wheat or graham flour for 1 cup white flour and mix with sifted dry ingredients. Increase salt to ¾ teaspoon.

GRAVY

¼ cup bacon grease
1 onion, diced
½ cup flour
½ teaspoon salt
1 teaspoon black pepper
2 cups milk

Sauté onion in bacon grease in a heavy saucepan on medium heat. Add flour, salt, and pepper and stir. Cook for 2 minutes; add milk and whisk to prevent lumps. Bring to a boil.

GARLIC CHEESE BREAD

1 loaf Italian bread
1 stick butter or margarine
2 cloves garlic, minced
1 teaspoon paprika
1 teaspoon black pepper
¼ cup chopped fresh parsley
1 cup shredded Mozzarella cheese

Preheat oven to 350 degrees. Split bread lengthwise and slice about every 2 or 3 inches. Do not slice through bottom crust. Place bread on rack above a cookie sheet.

Melt butter in saucepan and add garlic, paprika, and black pepper. Simmer a few minutes then spoon onto bread; let it soak in. Sprinkle cheese liberally on bread followed by a sprinkle of parsley for garnish. Bake at 350 degrees until bread is crusty and cheese is bubbly—about 10 minutes.

ONION CHEESE LOAF

1 loaf French bread
6 tablespoons butter or margarine
3 tablespoons prepared mustard
1 onion, thinly sliced
Sliced sharp processed American cheese

Cut bread diagonally at 1-inch intervals, cutting to but not through bottom crust. Blend butter and mustard and spread over cut surfaces. Insert a slice of cheese and a slice of onion in each slash.

Wrap loaf in foil; heat over medium coals 15 minutes or until heated, and cheese melts.

Yield: 1 loaf

ONION-CHEESE POPOVERS

1 cup flour
¾ teaspoon salt
½ teaspoon onion powder
3 eggs
1 cup milk
3 tablespoons melted butter or salad oil
1 cup grated Cheddar cheese

Preheat oven to 350 degrees. Sift together flour, salt, and onion powder. Beat together eggs, milk, and butter or oil; stir into dry ingredients just until well blended. Stir in grated cheese. Spoon batter into well-greased muffin tins, each about half full. Bake for 40 minutes at 350 degrees. Prick each popover with fork and allow steam to escape at end of baking time. Serve immediately.

Yield: 6 servings

YORKSHIRE PUDDING

4 eggs, beaten
2 cups milk
¾ cup butter or beef drippings
1¾ cups flour
1 teaspoon salt

Heat oven to 450 degrees. Combine eggs, milk, and 6 tablespoons of the melted butter or beef drippings; add flour and salt. Beat three minutes.

While beating, coat bottom and sides of ten 6-ounce custard cups with remaining butter or beef drippings. Place cups in oven to heat.

Beat batter constantly until custard cups are hot.

Pour immediately into cups, dividing batter evenly. Bake at 450 degrees for 10 minutes. Reduce oven temperature to 350 degrees and continue baking 20 minutes or until golden brown.

Yield: 10 servings

Note: Can be cooked in roasting pan and cut in squares.

GERMAN PANCAKES

½ cup butter
1 cup milk
1 cup flour
6 eggs
½ teaspoon salt

Melt butter in oven in 9x13-inch pan until bubbling. Mix all ingredients together and pour into hot butter. Bake at 450 degrees for 15 to 20 minutes or until golden brown. Serve with jams, syrup, powdered sugar, fresh lemon juice, etc., for breakfast or with meats for dinner.

Yield: 6 to 8 servings

WHOLE WHEAT PANCAKES
(Using Whole Kernel Wheat)

¾ cup whole-kernel wheat
¾ cup milk
1 egg

Combine ingredients in blender container and blend on medium to high speed for 4 minutes or until wheat mixture is smooth and creamy. Add:

¼ cup milk
1 egg
1 tablespoon honey
2 tablespoons oil
2 teaspoons baking powder
½ teaspoon salt
½ teaspoon soda

Add ingredients to wheat mixture and mix only until blended.
Bake immediately on hot griddle.

SOURDOUGH STARTER

1 package dry yeast
½ cup warm water
2 cups flour
2 cups lukewarm water
1 tablespoon sugar
1 teaspoon salt

Dissolve yeast in ½ cup warm water. Stir in flour, water, sugar, and salt. Let stand uncovered at room temperature for 3 to 5 days, stirring two or three times a day. Cover at night to prevent drying. Store in a covered plastic container or glass bowl in the refrigerator. Do not freeze.

SOURDOUGH PANCAKES

2 cups milk
2 cups flour
½ cup sourdough starter
1 teaspoon soda
1 teaspoon salt
4 teaspoons sugar
2 tablespoons shortening
2 eggs

Combine milk, flour, and starter in a bowl and mix well. Leave mixture uncovered on the counter overnight.

In the morning, take ½ cup mixture out to add to the starter in the refrigerator.

Add the rest of the ingredients to the remaining mixture and mix well.

Cook on griddle or frying pan.

BUTTERMILK ABLESKIVERS (CREPES)

5 eggs
1½ cups flour
2 cups buttermilk
1 teaspoon soda
Dash salt

Combine all ingredients, mix well, and cook as crepes in a small frying pan or crepe pan.

CIDER SYRUP

1 cup sugar
3 tablespoons baking mix (Bisquick)
1 teaspoon ground cinnamon
2 cups apple cider
2 tablespoons lemon juice
¼ cup margarine or butter

Mix sugar, baking mix, and cinnamon in 2-quart saucepan; stir in cider and lemon juice. Cook, stirring constantly, until mixture thickens and boils. Boil and stir 1 minute; remove from heat. Stir in margarine.

AUNT AMY'S PEACH SYRUP

Next time you bottle peaches, try this recipe using the peelings.

Peaches
Sugar
Maple flavoring

Wash peaches very well; peel and save peelings. Cover peelings with water and boil for 45 minutes in a covered pan. Strain in a colander, being careful not to press too hard. The liquid will be clear in color.

Add two parts peach juice to one part sugar. Boil slowly until mixture thickens to syrup consistency. Add a small amount of maple flavoring to taste.

Place in prepared containers. Will keep in refrigerator for 2 or 3 months.

HONEY BUTTER

Combine equal amounts of honey and butter or margarine in blender. Mix on low speed until well blended and fluffy. Add a few drops of vanilla, if desired.

Variation: Substitute raspberry jam for the honey.

QUICK 'N' EASY HERB SPREAD

1 pound cream cheese, softened
1 cup butter, softened
¼ teaspoon garlic powder
1 teaspoon oregano
½ teaspoon basil
½ teaspoon dill weed
½ teaspoon ground pepper
½ teaspoon marjoram

Cream together cheese and butter in bowl of mixer or food processor. Add herbs and mix well. Cover and chill 24 hours. Serve at room temperature as a spread on snack crackers or bread.

Yield: 3 cups

SAVORY BREAD TOPPING

½ cup corn flake crumbs
1 tablespoon parsley flakes
½ teaspoon garlic powder
½ cup Parmesan Cheese
2 tablespoons salad seasoning
1 tablespoon sesame seeds

Combine all ingredients and sprinkle over homemade or refrigerator bread sticks before baking.

May

Sweet Conclusions

One day when we went walking
I found a dragon's tooth,
A dreadful dragon's tooth,
"A locust thorn," said Ruth.

One day when we went walking,
I found a Brownie's shoe,
A Brownie's button shoe,
"A dry pea pod," said Sue.

One day when we went walking,
I found a mermaid's fan,
A merry mermaid's fan,
"A scallop shell," said Dan.

One day when we went walking,
I found a fairy's dress,
A fairy's flannel dress,
"A mullein leaf," said Bess.

Next time that I go walking,
Unless I meet an elf,
A funny, friendly elf,
I'm going by myself!
Valene Hobbs

Invitations

The invitation to a party will be the first indication to the guest about the type of affair it will be. Carry out the theme of the celebration with the invitation. It could be a formal printed invitation or a handwritten note, tied onto a bouquet of balloons or delivered with a single flower, filled with confetti or enclosed in a can. A phone call is always appropriate and allows you to know immediately if the guest can attend. Always include an RSVP on the invitation and make a follow-up call if necessary.

Fun Tips

Desserts can be enjoyed by everyone, not limited to the few that can indulge. Some simple suggestions are:

* ★ Lemon or orange halves hollowed out and filled with fruit sorbet.
* ★ Strawberries dipped in white and dark chocolate.
* ★ Cantaloupe wedges served with raspberries and lime.
* ★ Cold fruit soup.
* ★ Sliced peaches over vanilla ice cream.
* ★ A baked apple.
* ★ Sliced oranges sprinkled with powdered sugar.
* ★ Sliced bananas drizzled with maple syrup and lightly broiled.
* ★ Poached pears.

Graduation Brunch

Mixed fruit in a grapefruit shell

Cheese Strata (p. 7)

Fresh broccoli with lemon butter

Sticky Caramel Rolls (p. 82)

Nectarine Sorbet (p. 106)

White grape juice with lemon–lime carbonated beverage

Graduation Brunch

* Fashion mortarboard invitations and place cards by using construction paper.
* Use carnations the color of the school as a centerpiece (carnations can be dyed through the stem by using colored water).
* Use tablecloth and napkins in school colors.
* Tie a bow around a copy of a favorite poem, saying, advice, or date of graduation as a favor.
* Trace your hand and have graduates list the five funniest experiences they had or five wonderful things about another person in the room. Have each share their list with the group.

May Day

* Plan a May Day hike. Write a list of things to look for, i.e.: flower, bird, bee, butterfly, round rock, ant, feather,

birds nest, etc. Take a hammer to break rock and look for gold.

★ Make a May Pole cake.

Mothers Day

★ Everyone recount one thing they remember about Grandma and Mom and record it on paper. Add to the list each year.

Decoration Day

★ Time to remember the family genealogy by looking at names on the head stones.

★ Put flowers on the graves; find one that doesn't have any flowers and place some on it.

★ Come home and have a picnic and read your family history or relate a story about a relative.

★ Plant a family flower or vegetable garden.

Sweet Conclusions

Frozen Desserts

THELMA'S ICE CREAM

1 quart milk, heated
3½ cups sugar, dissolved in hot milk
3 cups mocha mix
6 oranges, juiced
1 can (10 ounces) reduced acid orange juice
6 junket tablets dissolved in a little hot tap water
1 can (8 ounces) crushed pineapple
1 bottle (6 ounces) maraschino cherries, chopped
1 to 2 tablespoons vanilla

Combine milk and sugar mixture with mocha mix, juice from oranges, and canned orange juice. Place in freezer to cool while preparing the rest of the ingredients. Combine dissolved junket, pineapple, cherries, and vanilla; add cooled orange juice mixture and process in ice cream freezer according to instructions.

Yield: 1 gallon

NECTARINE SORBET WITH RASPBERRY SAUCE

1 cup sugar
½ cup water
5 ripe nectarines, pared, pitted, cut into chunks
2 tablespoons fresh lime juice
2 tablespoons raspberry liqueur, preferably Chambord,
    or raspberry juice
1 teaspoon grated lime zest
Raspberry Sauce (recipe follows), optional

Heat sugar and the water in medium saucepan, stirring constantly, to boiling. Reduce heat to medium-low and simmer, stirring occasionally, until consistency is syrupy, about 10 minutes. Let cool to room temperature, then refrigerate until cold. Place nectarines and lime juice in food processor or blender and process until very smooth. Stir in raspberry liqueur or raspberry juice, lime zest, and syrup.

Freeze in ice cream maker according to manufacturer's instructions. Store in airtight container in freezer. Make Raspberry sauce, if using. To serve, scoop nectarine sorbet into bowls and pass raspberry sauce.

Yield: 1 quart

RASPBERRY SAUCE

1 package (10 ounces) frozen raspberries, thawed

Place berries in food processor and process until smooth. Press through fine sieve into serving bowl to remove seeds. Refrigerate until ready to serve.

Yield: 1 cup

FRESH BERRY ICE CREAM

5 eggs
2 cups sugar
¼ teaspoon salt
1 tablespoon vanilla
2 tablespoons lemon juice
2 cups whipping cream
    OR 1 cup whipping cream and 1 cup canned milk
1 quart milk
2½ cups sweetened fresh or frozen fruit (crushed or
    sliced strawberries, raspberries, peaches, blueberries,
    etc.)

Beat eggs until light and fluffy. Gradually add sugar, beating constantly until mixture is light and fluffy. Add salt, vanilla, and lemon juice. Beat; add cream, beat; add milk, beat. Pour into hand or electric freezer. When mixture begins to become frozen, stir in fruit and finish freezing.

Serve in cones for children or serve scoop of ice cream in dish using cones for hats. Decorate scoop of ice cream with candies to make a face. Small cookies can be ears.

Yield: 1 gallon

CINNAMON ICE CREAM

Serve over apple or pumpkin pie or a warm baked apple.

> 2 eggs
> 1 cup sugar
> 2 tablespoons ground cinnamon
> ⅛ teaspoon salt
> ½ box (3½ ounces) instant vanilla pudding
> 4 cups half and half
>   OR 2 cups half and half and 2 cups whipping cream
> 1 teaspoon vanilla extract

Beat eggs in mixing bowl until fluffy. Mix cinnamon and sugar together and add to eggs. Add remaining ingredients and continue beating until sugar and pudding dissolve. Pour mixture into cream can and churn-freeze according to manufacturer's directions.

MAURINE'S PARTY ICE CREAM

> 1 quart vanilla ice cream, softened
> 1 quart pineapple sherbet, softened
> 1 package (10 ounces) frozen strawberries, partially thawed
> 3 medium bananas, sliced, then quartered
> ¾ cup chopped pecans

Blend ice cream, sherbet, and fruit; add bananas and nuts. Return to freezer but remove about 45 minutes before serving. Garnish with fresh berries.

Yield: 2½ quarts

Note: Can substitute fresh peaches or other summer fruits for berries. Softening time before serving gives the taste and appearance of homemade ice cream, fresh from the freezer. Can be doubled and frozen for one month.

MAURINE'S HOLIDAY ICE CREAM

1 quart vanilla ice cream, softened
1 quart orange sherbet, softened
1 can coconut creme mix
1 large can crushed pineapple, drained
2 medium bananas, diced
¾ cup sliced almonds
Maraschino cherries, fresh mint leaves, mandarin
    oranges, and toasted coconut for garnish

Soften ice cream and sherbet; blend with coconut creme mix, crushed pineapple, bananas, and almonds. Return to freezer. Remove from freezer about 45 minutes before serving. Garnish as desired.

Yield: 2½ quarts

SNOWBALLS

½ gallon vanilla ice cream
Angel flake coconut
Chocolate sauce

Spoon vanilla ice cream into large, round ice cream balls; roll in coconut to coat. Place on cookie sheet and freeze until firm. Serve on a bed of chocolate sauce.

HOLIDAY PEPPERMINT FREEZE

1¼ cups finely crushed vanilla wafers (28 wafers)
4 tablespoons butter, melted
1 half gallon peppermint stick ice cream, softened
½ cup butter
2 squares (2 ounces) unsweetened chocolate
3 egg yolks, well beaten
1½ cups sifted powdered sugar
½ cup chopped pecans (optional)
1 teaspoon vanilla
3 egg whites

Toss together crumbs and melted butter. Reserve ¼ cup crumb mixture; press remaining crumb mixture into a 9x9-inch baking pan. Spoon ice cream onto crust; freeze. Melt ½ cup butter and the chocolate over low heat; gradually stir into egg yolks. Add powdered sugar, nuts, and vanilla. Beat until smooth. Cool thoroughly. Beat egg whites until stiff peaks form. Fold egg whites into chocolate mixture. Spread over ice cream; top with the reserved crumb mixture; freeze.

Yield: 8 servings

GRASSHOPPER SUNDAE

½ cup crushed pineapple and juice
1 cup sugar
½ cup light corn syrup
1 cup water
Dash of salt
Few drops green coloring
Peppermint flavoring or creme de menthe
Mint or maraschino cherries for garnish

Boil all the ingredients together—except flavoring—until pineapple is clear. Add a few drops of peppermint flavoring or creme de menthe and pour over vanilla ice cream. Garnish each dish with a sprig of mint. Or during the holiday season, place a maraschino cherry on top of the sundae for a gala red and green color combination.

Yield: 6 to 8 servings

TOPPENISH APPLE CAKE

2 cups sugar
½ cup oil
2 eggs
2 cups flour
2 teaspoons cinnamon
1 teaspoon salt
2 teaspoons soda
4 cups grated raw apples
1 cup chopped nuts

Combine all ingredients and mix well. Pour into a greased oblong pan and bake at 350 degrees for 40 to 45 minutes.

LINCOLN LOG ROLL

½ package of devil's food cake mix
⅓ cup water
3 eggs
Powdered sugar
½ cup chopped maraschino cherries
½ cup pecans
1 chocolate bar, grated
1 quart cherry pecan ice cream, softened
1 carton (8 ounces) frozen whipped topping, thawed
6 to 8 maraschino cherries

Combine cake mix, water, and eggs in medium bowl. Beat with mixer 1 minute until smooth. Pour batter into a jelly-roll pan lined with greased wax paper. Bake at 375 degrees for 12 to 15 minutes. Cool. Remove cake from pan onto a towel sprinkled with powdered sugar. Roll cake in towel and set aside.

Combine chopped cherries, pecans, ice cream, and half the grated chocolate in a bowl. Mix until ice cream is smooth. Unroll cake and spread ice cream mixture one inch from the edge. Roll without towel. Wrap cake roll in plastic wrap and freeze until firm. Before serving, allow cake roll to stand at room temperature 20 minutes. Garnish with whipped topping, grated chocolate, and cherries.

Yield: 6 to 8 servings

GHOST CAKE

Bake a sheet cake and frost with chocolate frosting. Make a ghost shape on the cake with white frosting. Place 2 empty eggshell halves where ghost's eyes would be. Place a sugar cube coated in lemon extract in each shell. When ready to serve, light sugar cubes.

Piña Colada Cake

1 yellow cake mix
1 bottle piña colada mixer
1 can (14 ounces) sweetened condensed milk
Coconut
1 container (8 ounces) frozen whipped topping, thawed

Bake cake as directed in an oblong pan. Let cool; pull apart with fork in the pan. Mix ½ bottle piña colada mixer and sweetened condensed milk; pour over cake. Sprinkle with coconut and frost with whipped topping. Let stand in refrigerator overnight.

Yield: 12 to 16 servings

Oatmeal Cake

1½ cups boiling water
1 cup quick oats
½ cup butter
2 eggs
1 cup brown sugar
1 cup white sugar
1 teaspoon soda
1 teaspoon nutmeg
1 teaspoon cinnamon
1⅓ cup flour
1 teaspoon vanilla

Pour water over oats. Add butter. Let stand until butter melts. Beat eggs; add brown sugar, white sugar, soda, nutmeg, cinnamon, flour, vanilla to eggs. Combine both mixtures and stir well. Bake in a well greased and floured pan at 350 degrees for 35 minutes. Frost with German chocolate cake frosting.

113

STRAWBERRY ANGEL TORTE

1 (9-inch) angel food cake
1 package (10 ounces) frozen strawberries, thawed
1 envelope unflavored gelatin
¼ cup sugar
2 tablespoons lemon juice
2 cups whipping cream
¼ teaspoon vanilla
Fresh strawberries for garnish

Split cake horizontally into 3 layers. Drain strawberries and combine juice with gelatin. Let stand one minute. Add sugar and lemon juice. Microcook 2 minutes until sugar and gelatin are dissolved. Refrigerate for 25 minutes. Combine gelatin mixture, strawberries, and vanilla. Beat at high speed of electric mixer until light and frothy. Whip cream and fold into strawberry mixture. Blend well.

Place one cake round on a serving plate. Spread with ⅓ of strawberry filling. Repeat with remaining cake layers and filling, ending with remaining filling on top of last layer. Refrigerate until ready to serve. Garnish with strawberry slices or chocolate dipped strawberries.

Yield: 16 servings

Filling variations for angel food cake:
#1
1 pint whipping cream, whipped and sweetened
2 cups marshmallow cream
1 can (15¼ ounces) crushed pineapple, drained

Combine all ingredients and gently blend. Place between cake layers.

#2

3 chocolate bars with almonds (4 ounces each)
1½ cups whipping cream, whipped
2 tablespoons sugar
1 teaspoon vanilla

Melt chocolate bars in top part of double boiler over boiling water or in microwave oven. Barely cool. While chocolate is cooling, whip cream (not too stiff). Mix in sugar and vanilla. Fold chocolate into the whipped cream until blended. Frost cake.

Note: If you would like to split cake in half or thirds and frost between layers, use four and a half rather than three 4-ounce chocolate bars and 2 cups (1 pint) whipping cream rather than 1½ cups.

RAZ-MA-TAZ

1 white cake mix with pudding in the mix
1 package raspberry Danish Dessert, prepared according to sauce recipe on the box (use raspberry juice as the liquid) cool
2 packages frozen raspberries with juice, partially thawed
1 package (8 ounces) cream cheese, softened
2 cups powdered sugar
1 pint whipping cream, whipped

Make cake according to package directions. Pour batter into 2 oblong pans or 1 large bundt pan. Bake at 350 degrees for 15 minutes. Beat cream cheese and sugar until creamy; fold in whipped cream. Spread evenly over cooled cakes. Gently fold raspberries into prepared raspberry sauce; spread on top of cream cheese layer.

Yield: 2 cakes

DATE CAKE

1½ cups sugar
1 cup salad oil
3 eggs
2 cups sifted flour
1 teaspoon baking soda
1 teaspoon salt
1 teaspoon nutmeg
1 teaspoon cinnamon
1 teaspoon allspice
1 cup buttermilk
1 cup chopped walnuts
1 cup pitted chopped dates
1 teaspoon vanilla extract
Buttermilk icing (recipe follows)

Combine sugar, oil, and eggs. Beat mixture until smooth and creamy. Sift together dry ingredients ; add alternately with buttermilk to creamed mixture. Mix until smooth. Stir in nuts, dates, and vanilla. Turn batter into a greased and floured oblong pan or bundt pan. Bake at 300 degrees for 55 to 60 minutes. Cool cake in pan for 15 minutes. Spread with icing. Cut into slices.

Yield: 24 servings

Buttermilk Icing:

1 cup sugar
½ cup buttermilk
½ teaspoon baking soda
½ teaspoon vanilla extract
½ cup butter or margarine

Combine ingredients in saucepan. Cook over medium heat, stirring constantly to soft ball stage. Remove from heat and cool 5 minutes. Beat mixture until it starts thickening. Pour at once over cake in pan.

Yield: About 1½ cups icing

ANY FRUIT CAKE

2 eggs
2 cups sugar
1 cup oil
5 cups flour
4 teaspoons cinnamon
2 teaspoons nutmeg
½ teaspoon salt
4 teaspoons baking soda
1 quart bottled fruit and juice (any kind)
1 cup chopped nuts

Cream eggs, sugar, and oil. Stir in dry ingredients; add fruit, juice, and nuts and mix well. Pour into a greased oblong pan and bake at 350 degrees for 40 to 50 minutes. Frost with a butter cream frosting.

Yield: 12 servings

BETTER THAN ANYTHING CAKE

1 package butter cake mix
4 eggs
½ cup oil
¼ cup water
1 package (4 ounces) instant vanilla pudding
1 cup sour cream
1 package (6 ounces) chocolate chips
½ cup chopped nuts

Combine cake mix, eggs, oil, water, pudding, and sour cream and mix well. Fold in chocolate chips and nuts. Pour into greased bundt pan. Bake at 350 degrees for 1 hour.

THELMA'S ICING

1 cup milk
3 tablespoons flour
1 cup butter or margarine
1 cup sugar
1 teaspoon vanilla

Combine milk and flour in a saucepan and cook on a medium temperature until thick and stiff; cool in the refrigerator. Whip butter and sugar together until whipped cream consistency. Add cooled milk mixture and vanilla and mix well with electric mixer.

BROILED ICING

¼ cup butter
½ cup brown sugar
3 tablespoons evaporated milk
¾ cup coconut
½ cup chopped nuts, if desired

Cream butter and sugar. Beat in milk; add coconut and nuts. Spread on hot cake; broil for 2 to 4 minutes.

CARAMEL ICING

1½ cups brown sugar
¼ cup milk
2 tablespoons butter
1 teaspoon vanilla

Combine sugar, milk, and butter; boil 3 minutes, stirring constantly. Add vanilla. Cool to lukewarm, beat.

MOCK APPLE PIE

¾ cup sugar, divided
⅛ teaspoon salt
1 tablespoon cornstarch
1 teaspoon grated lemon rind
1 tablespoon lemon juice
2 quarts pears, drained and quartered
1 unbaked pie shell
½ cup flour
½ teaspoon cinnamon
½ teaspoon ginger
½ teaspoon mace
¼ cup butter

Combine ¼ cup of the sugar, salt, cornstarch, rind, and lemon juice and spread over pears. Pour into an unbaked pie shell. Mix rest of sugar, flour, and spices; cut butter in until crumbly. Sprinkle over pie. Bake at 450 degrees for 15 minutes then lower temperature to 350 degrees and continue baking for an additional 30 minutes.

Yield: 1 pie

GEORGIA PEACH PIE

1 nut crunch pastry shell (recipe below)
1 package (10 ounces) large marshmallows
½ cup milk
1 cup whipping cream, whipped
1¾ to 2 cups peeled and sliced fresh peaches

In 3-quart casserole, place marshmallows and milk. Cover. Microcook on high 2 to 3 minutes, until mixture can be stirred smooth. Chill in refrigerator (about 30 to 40 minutes) until thickened, stirring occasionally.

Fold in whipped cream and fresh peaches. Pour into crust and decorate with reserved crumbs or additional whipped cream, if desired. Refrigerate several hours or overnight.

Yield: One 9-inch pie

NUT CRUNCH PASTRY SHELL

1 cup flour
½ cup light brown sugar
½ cup butter
1 cup chopped pecans or walnuts

In small mixing bowl, place flour and brown sugar. With pastry blender, cut in butter until mixture is crumbly. Mix in nuts.

Place crumbly mixture loosely in 9-inch pie plate. Microcook on high 4 to 5 minutes, stirring every 1 or 2 minutes. Stir again after cooking and, if desired, reserve about 2 tablespoons crumbly mixture to garnish top of pie. Press remainder of hot crumbs into pie plate. Microcook on high 2 to 3 minutes, until set, rotating dish ¼ turn every minute. Cool before filling.

Yield: One 9-inch pie shell

FROZEN LEMON PIE

1½ cups finely crushed vanilla wafers (36 wafers)
4 tablespoons butter, melted
1 half gallon vanilla ice cream, softened
½ can (12 ounce size) frozen lemonade concentrate,
    thawed

Toss together crushed wafers and melted butter. Reserve 3 tablespoons mixture for topping; press remaining mixture into a 9-inch square baking pan. Combine ice cream and lemonade and mix well. Spoon ice cream mixture onto crust, top with reserved crumbs and freeze until firm.

Variation: Add ½ cup finely chopped nuts to crumb
    mixture.

Yield: 8 servings

PIE CRUST

1 pound lard
5 cups flour
1½ teaspoons salt
1 egg
2 tablespoons vinegar
Cold water

Cut lard into flour and salt until mixture is crumbly. Crack egg into an 8-ounce measuring cup; add vinegar and fill cup with cold water to measure 8 ounces. Beat well. Add to flour mixture, mixing well. Can be stored a few weeks in the refrigerator.

GRAHAM CRACKER CRUST

12 graham crackers, crushed (1½ cups crumbs)
⅓ cup sugar
½ cup butter or margarine

Combine all ingredients and press into a greased 9 inch pie pan. Bake at 375 degrees for 45 minutes.

VANILLA WAFER CRUST

1¼ cups crushed vanilla wafers
1 tablespoon sugar
4 tablespoons butter or margarine, melted

Combine all ingredients; press into a 9-inch pie pan and bake at 375 degrees for 7 minutes.

CORN FLAKE CRUST

1 cup crushed corn flakes
¼ cup sugar
⅓ cup butter or margarine, melted

Combine all ingredients and press into a greased 9-inch pie pan. Chill until set.

BAKED CUSTARD

3 eggs
¼ to ½ cup sugar
¼ teaspoon salt
1 teaspoon vanilla
2 cups milk
Dash nutmeg

Combine eggs, sugar, salt, and vanilla and beat on high speed of mixer until thick. Add cold milk and beat on medium speed until well blended. Grease 6 custard cups; pour mixture in cups and place in an oblong pan with 3 cups of hot water. Bake at 325 degrees for 50 to 70 minutes. Cool custard cups on a wire rack.

Yield: 6 servings

FANCY BREAD PUDDING

3 eggs, beaten
¾ cup sugar
1 can (12 ounces) evaporated milk
1 cup milk
1 can (20 ounces) cooking apples
½ teaspoon nutmeg
½ teaspoon cinnamon
6 cups bread cubes (French bread, crust removed)
1 cup raisins or nuts, optional

Combine eggs, sugar, milks, and spices in 3 quart casserole; stir until blended. Add bread cubes, apples, and raisins, let stand until bread cubes become saturated. Microcook on medium setting for 20 to 25 minutes or until knife inserted in center comes out clean. Serve with whipped cream or ice cream, if desired.

Yield: 6 to 8 servings

HAWAIIAN RICE PUDDING

¾ cup crushed pineapple, drained
2 tablespoons lemon juice
⅓ cup sugar
⅛ teaspoon salt
1 cup whipping cream, whipped
2 cups cold cooked rice
½ cup shredded coconut

Combine pineapple, lemon juice, sugar, and salt. Fold mixture into whipped cream. Fold in rice and coconut. Chill.

Yield: 6 servings

HOT FUDGE PUDDING

1 cup flour
¾ cup sugar
1 tablespoon cocoa
2 teaspoons baking powder
¾ teaspoons salt
½ cup milk
2 tablespoons butter, melted
¼ cup nuts

Combine all ingredients and pour into a greased oblong pan. Sprinkle with topping; pour 1¾ cup boiling water over entire surface. Bake at 350 degrees for 40 minutes.

Yield: 10 to 12 servings

Topping:

1 cup sugar
2 tablespoons cocoa

CHERRY NUT PUDDING

1 cup sugar
1 cup flour
¼ teaspoon salt
1 egg, beaten
1 cup sweet cherries and juice
2 tablespoons melted butter
1 teaspoon soda, dissolved in 1 teaspoon water
1 cup nuts
sauce (recipe follows)

Combine sugar, flour, and salt; add egg and juice from cherries. Mix well. Add butter, soda, and water; blending well. Fold in cherries and nuts. Pour into a greased 11x7½ inch pan and bake at 400 degrees for 30 to 40 minutes. Serve with slightly sweetened whipped cream.

Yield: 4 to 6 servings

Sauce:

1 cup brown sugar
1 tablespoon butter
1 teaspoon vanilla
1 tablespoon flour
1 cup water
Pinch of salt

Boil until thick. Pour on pudding as soon as it comes from oven. (While sauce is still hot.)

CHRISTMAS CARROT PUDDING

    1 teaspoon baking powder
    1 teaspoon soda
    2 cups grated potatoes
    ½ cup raisins
    ½ cup currants
    ¼ pound suet or butter
    2 teaspoons cloves
    2 teaspoons cinnamon
    2 teaspoons allspice
    2 teaspoons nutmeg
    1 cup nuts
    2 cups grated carrots
    2 cups flour
    1 cup sugar
    1 cup brown sugar
    2 cups fine, dried bread crumbs
    ⅔ cup molasses

Dissolve baking powder and soda in grated potatoes. Mix all ingredients in the order given. Pack into can two-thirds full. Steam 2½ hours. Serve with Cream Sauce, Rum Sauce, or Lemon Sauce (recipes follow)

CREAM SAUCE

    1 cup sugar
    ½ teaspoon nutmeg
    ½ teaspoon salt
    2½ tablespoons flour
    2 cups boiling water
    1 cup whipping cream

Mix dry ingredients and add to boiling water. Boil 3 to 5 minutes or until thick. Add cream. Serve hot.

Rum Sauce

½ cup unsalted butter
1 cup sugar
¼ cup boiling water
1 egg, beaten
Rum, brandy, vanilla, or lemon flavoring to taste

Cream butter and sugar; beat in boiling water. Cook in a double boiler stirring constantly or in a microwave oven until sugar is dissolved. Stir a little syrup into egg, then pour slowly in syrup mixture. Stir for 2 to 3 minutes. Let cool, add flavoring. Serve warm.

Lemon Sauce

1 cup sugar
2 tablespoons cornstarch
2 cups boiling water
1 lemon, juice and rind
2 tablespoons butter

Combine sugar and cornstarch; add boiling water gradually, stirring constantly. Cook 8 to 10 minutes; add juice and rind. Serve hot.

FRUIT JUICE SAUCE (COOKED JUICE)

¼ to ⅓ cup sugar
3 tablespoons flour
⅛ teaspoon salt
¾ cup hot water
¾ cup fruit juice
½ teaspoon vanilla or lemon extract

Mix sugar, flour, and salt thoroughly. Pour the hot water into sugar mixture. Blend thoroughly. Tiny lumps disappear as rapidly as mixture is heated and stirred. Cook, stirring constantly until thickened and flour taste has disappeared. Cover and simmer about 5 minutes. Remove from heat; add fruit juice and flavoring. Serve cold or warm.

Substitutions and Variations:

2 tablespoons cornstarch may replace the flour.
1 teaspoon lemon juice and ½ teaspoon lemon rind
    may be used for flavoring.
Crushed or diced cooked fruit may be added with the
    fruit juice.
Canned or dried fruit juices are excellent used this way.

HOT FUDGE SAUCE

1 package (6 ounces) chocolate chips
½ cup evaporated milk

Combine chips and milk in a saucepan; cook over low heat, stirring constantly until chocolate melts completely.

Yield: 1 cup

CARAMEL SAUCE

½ cup brown sugar
1 tablespoon cornstarch
Dash salt
1 cup boiling water
2 tablespoons butter
1 teaspoon vanilla

Combine dry ingredients in a saucepan; add water and cook, stirring until clear and thickened. Remove from heat and add butter and vanilla.

Serve warm over ice cream or angel food cake.

SOFT CUSTARD SAUCE

2 cups milk
⅓ cup sugar
4 large egg yolks
1 teaspoon vanilla

Scald milk in a double boiler or in a microwave oven. Mix sugar with egg yolks; stir in some of the hot milk, then pour into pan. Cook, stirring constantly until custard thickens enough to coat the back of a metal spoon, about 15 to 20 minutes. Stir in vanilla. Cool, cover, and chill.

Serve over berries, oranges, or sponge cake.

Yield: 2¼ cups

APPLE-RHUBARB CRISP

1 egg
2 tablespoons flour
1 cup sugar
1 cup heavy cream
1 pound rhubarb, diced
2 apples, sliced

For topping:

1 cup brown sugar
1 cup flour
½ cup butter, softened

Beat egg, then add flour, sugar, and cream. Mix with rhubarb and apples, and place in a deep baking dish about 8 inches in diameter. Mix brown sugar, flour, and butter until crumbly and sprinkle over rhubarb mixture. Bake at 375 degrees for 30 minutes and serve warm or cold with whipped cream.

TRIFLE

1 package angel food cake mix
2 packages (3 ounces each) raspberry-flavored gelatin
2 packages (4 ounces each) vanilla pudding mix (not instant)
2 packages (10 ounces each) frozen raspberries or strawberries
½ cup sherry or red wine (optional)
1 container (8 ounces) frozen whipped topping or whipped heavy cream

Prepare and bake angel food cake according to package directions; cool. Cut in 3 layers. Prepare raspberry gelatin according to package directions; refrigerate. Prepare vanilla pudding mix according to package directions; refrigerate. When raspberry gelatin begins to set, whisk vigorously until light and frothy. In a deep clear glass bowl, place first angel food cake layer torn in pieces; cover with one third of raspberry gelatin. Thaw fruit, pour sherry or wine over fruit; drain, reserving juice-wine mixture. Top gelatin layer with one-third of the fruit then spread with a third of the vanilla pudding. Repeat next two layers. Pour juice-wine mixture over all and top with whipped topping or whipped heavy cream. Refrigerate overnight to set.

PUMPKIN DESSERT

1 large pumpkin
4 cups peeled chopped apples
2 cups raisins
2 cups nuts, chopped
2 teaspoons lemon juice
½ teaspoon cinnamon
½ teaspoon nutmeg
1 cup sugar
Whipped cream for garnish

Preheat oven to 350 degrees. Hollow out pumpkin, save top, wash and dry. Put all ingredients in pumpkin; mix. Put top on, place on a cookie sheet. Bake for at least 40 minutes or until apples are tender. Could take as long as an 1 hour and 45 minutes. Serve with whipped cream.

CHERRY CHEESECAKE TARTS

2 packages (8 ounces each) cream cheese
½ cup sugar
2 tablespoons lemon juice
2 eggs, beaten
1 teaspoon vanilla
1 teaspoon grated lemon rind
1 package vanilla wafers
1 can cherry pie filling

Mix cream cheese, sugar, lemon juice, rind, eggs, and vanilla. Beat until smooth and fluffy. Place cupcake liners in muffin tins. Place a vanilla wafer (flat side down) in each. Fill with cream cheese mixture, ½ to ¾ full. Bake at 350 degrees for 20 minutes. Remove from pans when cool. Top with cherry pie filling.

Yield: 2 to 2½ dozen tarts

LEMON CHARLOTTE

2 envelopes unflavored gelatin
½ cup cold water
6 egg yolks
½ cup sugar
½ cup lemon juice
6 egg whites
½ cup sugar
½ teaspoon cream of tartar
1 cup heavy cream
2 dozen ladyfingers
Fresh mint leaves

Dissolve gelatin in cold water. Beat egg yolks in large glass bowl until pale yellow. Add sugar, gelatin mixture and lemon juice. Microcook three minutes, stirring after each minute. Cool. Beat egg whites until soft peaks form. Gradually add ½ cup sugar and cream of tartar. Beat until stiff and glossy. Fold egg whites into egg yolk mixture. Whip cream until soft peaks form. Fold in egg mixture. Butter bottom of a spring-form pan and line bottom and sides with ladyfingers. Spoon filling into pan. Refrigerate at least four hours. Before serving, remove side from pan. Place charlotte on round serving plate. Garnish with mint leaves.

Yield: 8 servings

CHOCOLATE ECLAIR PIE

1 small box graham crackers
2 packages (3 ounces each) instant French vanilla pudding
3½ cups milk
1 carton (9 ounces) frozen whipped topping

Butter bottom and sides of an oblong pan and line with whole graham crackers. Mix pudding with milk. Blend in whipped topping. Layer pudding and crackers, ending with crackers.

Frosting:

2 packages ready-mix liquid chocolate
1 tablespoon white corn syrup
1½ cups powdered sugar
1 teaspoon vanilla
3 tablespoons milk
3 tablespoons melted butter

Mix all ingredients together until smooth. Carefully spread over graham crackers. Chill 24 hours.

Yield: 16 servings

POTS DE CREME

1½ envelopes (1½ tablespoons) unflavored gelatin
⅔ cup boiling water
1 package (6 ounces) chocolate chips
2 tablespoons sugar
Dash of salt
1 teaspoon vanilla
2 egg yolks
2 cups ice cubes
1 cup heavy cream

Place gelatin and boiling water in blender jar. Cover and blend about 40 seconds. Add chocolate chips, sugar, salt, vanilla, and egg yolks. Cover and blend 10 seconds. Add ice cubes and cream. Cover and blend 20 seconds or until it begins to thicken. Pour into small cups.

Yield: 6 to 8 servings

BAKED APPLES

1 cup brown sugar
1 cup water
2 tablespoons butter
½ teaspoon cumin
1 teaspoon cinnamon
¼ teaspoon mace
3 tablespoons vinegar
6 baking apples, cored

Combine all ingredients except apples and bring to a boil. Place apples in baking pan and cover with hot syrup. Bake uncovered at 350 degrees for 60 minutes, basting every 15 minutes. Serve warm with cream.

Yield: 6 servings

FRESH PEACH COBBLER

Filling:

4 to 5 cups fresh peaches (sliced and peeled)
1 scant cup granulated sugar
1 teaspoon grated lemon peel
1 tablespoon lemon juice
Pinch of salt
¼ teaspoon almond extract
¼ to ½ teaspoon ground nutmeg

Mix all of the above ingredients together in a deep dish casserole. Bake at 400 degrees while you make cobbler crust or until mixture is hot and bubbly.

Note: If using canned or frozen peaches, decrease sugar to ¼ cup.

Cobbler Crust:

1½ cups flour
3 teaspoons baking powder
¼ teaspoon salt
1 tablespoon granulated sugar
⅓ cup cold butter or shortening
1 egg
½ cup milk
granulated sugar
ground cinnamon

Sift together flour, baking powder, salt, and sugar. Cut in cold butter, using a pastry blender or two knives, into small, uniform pieces. In a liquid measuring cup beat egg; add milk. Stir into flour mixture until moistened, mixing lightly. Drop dough by spoonfuls over the hot peach mixture, spreading gently with a fork to cover completely. Sprinkle with sugar and cinnamon. Bake cobbler at 400 degrees for 25 to 30 minutes or until crust is done in the middle. Serve with whipped cream or ice cream.

Note: Crust recipe can be doubled for a thicker crust.

TINTED COCONUT

Place coconut in a glass jar. (Do not fill jar more than half full.) Dilute 2 or 3 drops of food coloring in 2 tablespoons water and sprinkle over coconut. Cover jar and shake until coloring is evenly distributed and desired shade is obtained. Sprinkle coconut on paper toweling to absorb any excess moisture.

Note: If desired, coconut may be tinted orange with grated orange rind. Use 1½ teaspoons grated orange rind to 1 cup coconut. Same procedure as above.

June

For Starters

I'll tell you how the Sun rose—
A Ribbon at a time.

Emily Dickinson

Music

After all is said and done, music adds that final touch to a social affair that says you've thought of everything. It cements all aspects of the party and conveys the theme instantly. It can soothe, add whimsy and frivolity, be dramatic, or add elegance. It is always sure to automatically put your guests at ease and entice conversation. Tapes and records can be checked out from the library.

Some ideas are:

* ★ Quiet piano music for Valentines' day.
* ★ Irish ballads for St. Paddy's Day.
* ★ Chamber or classical music for formal dinner parties.
* ★ Cowboy songs for a barbecue.
* ★ Patriotic tunes for the Fourth of July.
* ★ Musical scores for after-theater dessert.

* Oriental melodies for wok dinners.
* Spooky music for Halloween.
* College football songs for tailgate parties.
* Nutcracker Suite for holiday get together.

Summer Grill

Gazpacho Soup (p. 55) or

Cold Lemon Soup (p. 54)

Steak Pitas (p. 246)

Baked Beans (p. 210)

Fruit Plate with
Lemon Yogurt Dip (p. 154)

Chocolate Eclair Pie (p. 134) or

Piña Colada Cake (p. 113)

Minted Lemonade (p. 198)

Fun Tips

Fathers are sometimes hard to buy for. Consider these ideas:

* A picture book of his life.
* A poem run as an ad in the family section or sports section of the Sunday paper.
* Washing and waxing the car.
* Summer sausage (p. 232)
* Savory pretzels (p. 232)
* Herb spread (p. 100)
* Orange glazed pecans (p. 43)
* Chocolate dipped cookies, strawberries, or cashews

"Schools Out!"

* Tie a sandwich, fruit, and a cookie in a bandanna and secure on a stick to carry outside or to the park for a picnic.
* Organize a neighborhood play from a favorite book or story.
* Have a children's talent show or pet show.
* Rent a movie and show it outside—don't forget the popsicles and pink popcorn.

Fathers' Day

* Tell a story about a famous father, i.e., composer, father of our country, etc.
* Recall favorite memories of your father and grandfathers. Record them on paper. Add to the list each year.

For Starters

Appetizers

BACON-WRAPPED WHOLE WATER CHESTNUTS

3 to 4 cans (8 ounces each) whole water chestnuts
1 to 2 pounds bacon
Sauce (recipe follows)

Drain water chestnuts. Cut bacon slices in thirds. Wrap bacon pieces around chestnuts; fasten with a toothpick. Place in a 9x13-inch baking pan and bake at 350 degrees for 45 minutes. Pour sauce over and return to 350 degree oven for 20 minutes. Serve immediately.

Sauce

½ cup ketchup
⅓ cup brown sugar

In small saucepan, combine ketchup and brown sugar; bring to boil.

GARDEN DEVILED EGGS

6 eggs, hard boiled
¼ cup garlic and herb cheese spread
2 tablespoons mayonnaise
2 tablespoons finely chopped scallions
1 tablespoon finely chopped pimentos
1 tablespoon dijon mustard
48 wheat crackers
Parsley and tomato for garnish

Cut each egg crosswise in slices. Scoop yolks out into small bowl; mash well. Set egg whites aside. Stir cheese spread, mayonnaise, scallions, pimentos, and mustard into yolks until smooth and well blended. Top each cracker with an egg white slice. Spoon or pipe yolk mixture onto egg whites. Garnish with parsley and tomato if desired.

GRENADINE GRAPEFRUIT

2 cans (16 ounces each) grapefruit sections
1 can (17¼ ounces) pear halves, cut in chunks
2 apples, peeled and grated
3 tablespoons grenadine syrup
2 cups lemon–lime soda
Maraschino cherries
Lime twists

In a medium bowl, combine grapefruit, pear chunks, and grated apples. Spoon fruit into dessert glasses. Add grenadine syrup to the lemon–lime soda and pour over fruit. Garnish with cherries or lime twists.

Yield: 9 servings

APPETIZER PIE

1 9-inch frozen pie shell
1 package (3 ounces) cream cheese
½ cup mayonnaise
Cooked crumbled bacon
Black olives, sliced
Green olives, sliced
Mushrooms, sliced
Parsley, chopped

Defrost pie shell. Remove from tin and flatten on cookie sheet leaving fluted edge. Prick bottom with fork. Bake at 400 degrees for 8 to 10 minutes or until brown.

Mix cream cheese and mayonnaise together. Spread over cooled crust. Arrange bacon around the outer edge in ring shape. Arrange sliced mushrooms overlapping next to bacon, again in ring shape. Continue in the same manner with olives, ending with parsley in the center. Refrigerate and serve in wedges.

Yield: 1 pie

CHEESE TOAST

1 can (4 ounces) diced green chilis
½ cup butter
Dash garlic powder
1½ cups shredded Monterey Jack cheese
1¼ cups mayonnaise
6 small buns, sliced in half

In blender container, combine chilis, butter, and garlic powder. Mix well. Add cheese and mayonnaise.

Toast cut side of each bun half. Cut into small slices. Spread with cheese mixture and broil until bubbly.

Holiday Cheese Ball

2 packages (8 ounces each) cream cheese
1 can (8½ ounces) crushed pineapple, drained
2 cups chopped pecans
¼ cup chopped green pepper
2 tablespoons chopped onion
1 tablespoon seasoned salt
Pineapple slices
Maraschino cherries
Parsley

Soften cream cheese; gradually stir in crushed pineapple, 1 cup pecans, green peppers, onion, and salt. Chill well. Form into a ball and roll in 1 cup pecans. Chill until served. Garnish with twists of pineapple slices, maraschino cherries, and parsley. Serve with assorted crackers.

Miniature Cheese Balls

1 package (8 ounces) cream cheese, softened
1 can broken shrimp
¼ small onion, finely chopped
Chopped pecans

Combine cream cheese, shrimp, and onion and mix well. Divide mixture into small balls and roll in nuts.

CHEESY LOG

2 packages (8 ounces each) cream cheese
1 jar Old English cheese spread
½ pound blue cheese
½ pound finely shredded cheese
2 tablespoons grated onion
¼ teaspoon salt
Chopped pecans

Combine all ingredients except pecans and mix well. Form mixture in a log and roll in pecans.

CRAB CHEESE BALL

1 package (8 ounces) cream cheese
1 can (6½ ounces) crab meat, drained and flaked
2 tablespoons lemon juice
2 tablespoons horseradish
1½ tablespoons grated onion
2 teaspoons snipped chives
Dash Worcestershire sauce
¼ teaspoon salt
¼ cup minced black olives
Finely chopped walnuts or pecans

In medium bowl, place cream cheese, crab meat, lemon juice, horseradish, onion, chives, Worcestershire sauce, salt, and black olives. Blend well. Chill about 30 minutes. Shape into a large cheese ball or individual 1-inch cheese balls. Roll in finely chopped nuts. Serve with crackers.

Yield: One large or 30 individual balls

CHEESE BALL

1 package (8 ounces) cream cheese
1 package dry cheese sauce mix
Chopped pecans

Mix cream cheese and cheese sauce. Roll in pecans.

HOT CHEESE PUFFS

⅓ cup each: shredded Parmesan, sharp Cheddar, and
    Swiss cheeses
1 tube ready-to-bake biscuits
½ cup butter or margarine, melted
Paprika

Mix the cheeses. Cut each biscuit into quarters with sharp knife and roll in butter, then in cheese mixture. Coat well. Place on baking sheet, sprinkle with paprika and bake in very hot oven (450 degrees) 8 minutes or until golden brown and puffy. Serve piping hot with toothpicks.

Yield: 40 puffs

CHEESE STRAWS

1 stick of packaged pie pastry
1 cup shredded cheese (sharp cheddar)
Dash red pepper
Salt to taste

Follow directions on box for amount of water to add to pastry. Add the cheese and mix well. Season with red pepper and salt to suit taste. Press in strips from cookie press into desired lengths. Cook at 350 degrees for 15 to 20 minutes.

GOLD COINS

1 cup flour
¼ pound (1 cube) butter
1 cup shredded Cheddar Cheese
Pinch salt

Cut butter into flour with pastry cutter (or two knives) to consistency of corn meal. Add one cup shredded Cheddar Cheese with a pinch of salt and knead mixture until well blended. Form the dough into walnut-sized balls and bake on a greased cookie sheet in a 450 degree oven for 12 to 15 minutes until brown.

Yield: Approximately 4 dozen puffs

CHEESE BRAMBLES

½ cup butter or margarine
1 package (3 ounces) cream cheese
1 cup flour
¼ teaspoon salt
Dash cayenne pepper
5 slices American cheese

Mix butter and cream cheese together until smooth and creamy. Gradually add flour, salt, and pepper; blend until smooth.
Chill thoroughly. Roll dough to ⅛ inch thick and cut into 2-inch rounds. Lay a small piece of American cheese on one half of each round; fold over and crimp edges together with a fork. Chill until time to bake. Bake at 450 degrees for 8 to 10 minutes or until puffed and slightly brown.
Note: A small can of deviled ham could be substituted for the cheese.

Yield: About 3 dozen

CHILI CON QUESO

1 pound Velveeta cheese—cut into cubes
1 can (4 ounces) diced green chilis
1 can (1 pound) whole tomatoes, drained, then
    chopped fine
1 tablespoon dried minced onion

Heat all ingredients together in chafing dish over boiler pan until cheese is melted and it is hot.
Serve with corn chips.

EXPRESS CON QUESO DIP

1 pound Velveeta cheese, cubed
½ cup picante sauce

Combine ingredients and heat slowly, stirring frequently, just until cheese is melted. Serve with chips or vegetable dippers.

LAYERED MEXICAN DIP

Refried beans
Guacamole
Sour cream
Shredded Cheddar Cheese
Chopped tomatoes
Sliced olives

Layer ingredients in order listed on a serving dish. Serve with tortilla chips.

CHILI DIP

1 pound ground beef
1 medium onion, chopped
1 can (10 ounces) chili beef soup
1 can stewed tomatoes
1 can refried beans
1 cup shredded cheddar cheese
8 black olives, sliced
2 green onions, sliced

Brown the ground beef in 300 degree frying pan. Drain the grease. Add the onion, soup, tomatoes, and beans. Stir to combine. Turn the temperature dial down to medium low and warm for 10 to 15 minutes. Top with cheese, olives, and green onions before serving. Serve warm from the frying pan with tortilla and/or corn chips.

Variation: to make a casserole add the tortilla or corn chips after the rest of the ingredients and warm for 10 to 15 minutes.

Yield: 5½ cups

VEGETABLE DIP

1 quart mayonnaise (not salad dressing)
½ teaspoon dry mustard
1½ tablespoons tarragon vinegar
1 can anchovies
1 clove garlic, minced
½ cup chopped fresh parsley
8 capers

Combine all ingredients in blender container and mix well. Serve well chilled.

CLAM DIP

1 package (8 ounces) cream cheese
¼ cup mayonnaise
⅛ teaspoon garlic powder
¼ teaspoon onion salt
1 teaspoon lemon juice
1 can (6½ ounces) minced clams

Soften cream cheese. Mix together with mayonnaise until smooth. Add garlic powder, onion salt, and lemon juice. Fold in minced clams.

Serve with bread sticks or cut-up vegetables.

Yield: Approximately 1¾ cups

CHEESY ARTICHOKE DIP

1 can (4 ounces) diced green chilis
1 jar marinated artichoke hearts
½ cup shredded Parmesan cheese
½ cup mayonnaise

Combine all ingredients in a casserole dish and heat slowly. Serve with tortilla or corn chips.

WRANGLER DIP

1 can chili without beans
2 packages (8 ounces each) cream cheese
Dash chili powder

Combine chili and cream cheese and heat. Top with chili powder. Serve with tortilla or corn chips.

Avocado Cheese Dip

1 medium avocado
1 tablespoon lemon juice
1 cup small curd cottage cheese
½ cup dairy sour cream
½ teaspoon horseradish
½ teaspoon salt
¼ teaspoon Worcestershire sauce
Dash of cayenne pepper

Cut avocado in half; remove seed and skin. Force avocado through sieve or mash with fork; stir in lemon juice. Add remaining ingredients; blend. Chill. Serve with fresh vegetables or citrus fruit.

Fiesta Dip

1 jar chili sauce (homemade is great)
2 cans green chili salsa
1 can (4 ounces) diced green chilis (optional)
1 teaspoon chopped onion
2 avocados, finely diced

Combine all ingredients except avocados and refrigerate. Just before serving add avocados. Serve with tortilla chips.

ORANGE FRUIT DIP

1 egg, beaten
½ cup sugar
1 tablespoon orange peel
1 tablespoon lemon juice
1 cup whipping cream, whipped

Combine egg, sugar, orange peel, and lemon juice and heat for 5 minutes. Cool. Fold cooled mixture into whipped cream.

LEMON YOGURT DIP

1 carton (8 ounces) lemon-flavored yogurt
1 cup heavy cream, whipped
1 tablespoon sugar
1 teaspoon fresh grated lemon peel (optional)
Assorted fresh fruit

Pour yogurt into mixing bowl; gently fold in whipped cream. Add sugar and lemon peel; stir until blended. Serve with assorted fresh fruit.

July

Star-Spangled Salads

It takes four men to dress a salad:
a wise man for the salt, a madman for the pepper,
a miser for the vinegar, and a spendthrift for the oil.

Anonymous

Picnics

Originally the word "picnic" denoted a combined meal with each dish donated by a different guest. By the late eighteenth century the meaning had changed to indicate an elaborate meal of hot and cold dishes eaten outside. In the Victorian era, in the nineteenth century, the picnic allowed a proper place for men and women to mingle and laugh outside the confines of the restrictive house rules.

Fun Tips

Put strawberries, raspberries, or grapefruit in tossed summer salads for added color and flavor. Nasturtiums also work well, and can be eaten.

Use a variety of containers for salads—clean clay pots, footed trifle bowl, fried tortilla shells, clear glass bowls, and hollowed out watermelon.

Try a variety of "greens" in your green salads—watercress, endive, bibb lettuce, and spinach.

Use fruits and vegetables as containers for food—red cabbage for vegetable dips, oranges for sherbet, lemons for fruit dips, and melons for cold soups.

Patriotism and Pioneers
Happy Birthday America

Fresh Vegetable Platter with
Avocado Cheese Dip (p. 153)

Sloppy Joes (p. 14)

Red, White, and Blue Salad (p. 174)

Chips

Any Fruit Cake (p. 117)

Maurine's Holiday Ice Cream (p. 109)

Homemade Rootbeer (p. 203)

Fourth of July

* Decorate the outside of the house with streamers, lights, and balloons.
* Gather the family around early in the morning and have a flag ceremony to put up the flag.
* Assemble a children's "kitchen band" with kitchen utensils, gourd rattles, wooden rhythm sticks, bells, drum, triangle, and cymbals. Have a parade up and down the street.
* Construct paper hats out of newspapers or colored paper.
* Take your electric frying pan or griddle to the backyard for an outdoor breakfast.
* Ask someone to read the Declaration of Independence.
* Play round robin games—lawn darts, jacks, checkers, hopscotch, tiddly winks, old maid, trivia. Ring a bell when its time to rotate.
* Make "crackers" from empty toilet paper rolls—fill with candy and small surprises and wrap with colored foil or tissue paper and tie ends with ribbon.
* Make a "candle" centerpiece with a paper towel roll and decorate.
* Play patriotic music during dinner.
* Read pioneer stories.

Vacations

* Assemble a travel activity bag complete with car games, song book and quiet activities.
* Collect rocks, driftwood etc. on your vacation and paint them with messages or pictures and use them as paperweights.

Star-Spangled Salads

SPINACH SALAD

1 pound spinach, washed and blotted dry
1 can (11 ounces) mandarin oranges, drained
1 Bermuda onion, thinly sliced
½ cup pecans, browned in butter
⅓ cup red wine vinegar
½ cup oil
½ cup sugar
1 teaspoon dry mustard
½ teaspoon poppy seeds
1½ teaspoons minced onion

Combine vinegar, oil, sugar, mustard, poppy seeds, and minced onions in a sealed container, and shake to mix well. Refrigerate at least 2 hours.

Tear spinach into pieces and place in a large bowl. Top with oranges, onion, and pecans.

Just before serving, toss with dressing

Note: Sliced onions could be marinated in dressing. Can also add fresh strawberries and omit onion.

Yield: 6 servings

CITRUS SALAD

1 head red lettuce
½ Burmuda (Purple) onion, thinly sliced
3 oranges, peeled and thinly sliced
½ cup walnuts, sautéed in butter

Tear red lettuce and toss with onion, oranges, and walnuts. Top with dressing.

Dressing
½ cup sugar
1 teaspoon salt
½ teaspoon dry mustard
½ teaspoon celery seed
½ teaspoon poppy seed
½ medium onion, grated
¼ cup plus 2 tablespoons vinegar
1 cup oil

Mix well in blender. Let stand at least one day. Keeps two weeks. Good on any fruit salad.

Yield: 8 servings

SHEILA'S BROCCOLI SALAD

3 pounds broccoli, washed and drained
8 to 10 slices bacon, cooked until crisp
½ Bermuda onion
½ cup raisins
1 cup mayonnaise
¼ cup sugar
2 tablespoons vinegar

Cut broccoli flowerettes off stalks, reserving stalks for later use. Combine broccoli, bacon, onion, and raisins in a serving bowl. Combine mayonnaise, sugar, and vinegar and mix well. Pour over broccoli mixture and toss well. Refrigerate several hours.

Yield: 6 servings

JELLIED SOUR CREAM CUCUMBER SALAD

1 cup finely diced cucumber, seeded and peeled
1 teaspoon salt
Dash of pepper
1 envelope gelatin
¼ cup cold water
1 cup sour cream
3 tablespoons vinegar
2 tablespoons minced chives

Season cucumber with salt and pepper. Dissolve gelatin in ¼ cup cold water. Add sour cream, vinegar, chives, and cucumbers and mix well. Pour into molds.

Yield: 6 servings

BEAN SALAD

1 can (20 ounces) garbanzo beans, drained and rinsed
1 can (15½ ounces) red kidney beans, drained
1 can (16 ounces) baby lima beans, drained
1 can (16 ounces) cut green beans, drained
1 can (16 ounces) cut yellow wax beans, drained
1 medium-sized green pepper, minced
1 medium-sized onion, minced
⅓ cup salad oil
1 cup sugar
1½ cups vinegar
1 can french-fried onion rings
Lettuce leaves

In a large bowl combine all beans, green pepper and onion. In a jar with a lid, combine the oil, sugar, and vinegar; shake until thoroughly combined. Pour over bean mixture and toss lightly but thoroughly. Refrigerate for 2 hours. Just before serving, toss onion rings into mixture. Spoon into bowl lined with lettuce leaves.

Yield: 10 servings

GARDEN POTATO SALAD

3 pounds red potatoes
1½ cups finely sliced green onions (including tops)
About ⅛ cup dill pickle juice
    OR ¼ cup Italian dressing, optional
1¼ cups diced dill pickle
1 cup diced celery
1 cup sliced radishes (1 bunch)
1 cup (packed) finely chopped fresh parsley (less if
    preferred)
¾ to 1 cup chopped English cucumber
⅔ cup chopped green pepper (1 medium)
4 hard-boiled eggs
1 tablespoon salt, or to taste
1½ cups mayonnaise (approximately)
Sliced eggs, radishes, and cherry tomatoes for garnish
    (optional)

Boil potatoes in skins in salted water. Remove skins when still slightly warm. Dice potatoes, but not too fine (about a half-inch dice). If potatoes are rather dry, you may want to add pickle juice. Or, to make it more tangy, you may add Italian dressing, if desired.

Add pickle, celery, radishes, parsley (the parsley makes it!), cucumber, and green pepper. Reserve 4 slices hard-boiled egg for garnish. Dice rest into salad. Add salt and mayonnaise to taste, mixing well. (After it stands, you may want to add a little more mayonnaise or Italian dressing.) Garnish salad with reserved egg slices and radishes or cherry tomatoes, if desired.

Yield: 12 to 15 servings

TOMATO-ASPIC MOLDS

You can hollow out the bottom of each and fill with a surprise of cottage cheese or baby shrimp!

2 cups tomato juice
1 small bay leaf
3 or 4 whole cloves
2 slices onion
Salt and pepper
1 teaspoon lemon juice, fresh or frozen
1 tablespoon (1 envelope) unflavored gelatin
¼ cup cold water

Simmer tomato juice, bay leaf, cloves, and onion 5 minutes; strain; add seasonings and lemon juice. Soften gelatin in cold water; dissolve in hot mixture. Pour into individual molds. Chill until firm. Unmold on crisp endive. Garnish top with dollop of mayonnaise or salad dressing.

Yield: 6 servings

PICNIC RICE SALAD

1 cup long grain rice
2 cups mayonnaise
2 cups diced celery
1 small onion, finely chopped
4 teaspoons prepared mustard or mustard pickle relish
½ teaspoon salt
4 eggs, hard-boiled and chopped
8 radishes, sliced
1 cucumber, pared and diced

Cook rice according to package directions. Transfer to a large bowl. Cover and chill. Add mayonnaise, celery, onion, mustard, and salt to chilled rice. Mix well. Cover and chill. Stir in remaining ingredients just before serving.

Yield: 6 to 8 servings

FRUITED CHICKEN SALAD

2 cups uncooked shell macaroni
1 cup cole slaw salad dressing (Kraft)
1 cup mayonnaise
4 cups cooked chicken or turkey, diced
1 can (20 ounces) pineapple tidbits, drained
2 cups seedless grapes
2 cups diced apples
2 cups chopped celery
1 cup chopped almonds
Salt to taste

Cook macaroni, drain, and cool. Combine dressing and mayonnaise and add to macaroni. Mix well and refrigerate several hours or overnight. Just before serving add rest of the ingredients.

Yield: Sixteen 1-cup servings

CIOPPINO SALAD

1 medium Bermuda onion, sliced into rings
1 package (10 ounces) frozen peas, thawed
1 jar (6 ounces) marinated artichoke hearts, drained
1 can (4½ ounces) medium shrimp, rinsed and drained
1 tomato, cut into wedges
1 head iceberg lettuce
1½ cups diced celery
1½ cups imitation crab legs
Louis dressing (recipe below)

Break off six lettuce leaves and arrange on oval platter. Tear remaining lettuce into small pieces and place in a large bowl. Add onion rings, celery, peas, and artichoke hearts. Toss well. Spoon mixture onto platter. Place small pieces of crab and shrimp on top of lettuce mixture. Garnish with tomato wedges. Serve Louis dressing on the side.

Louis Dressing

1 cup mayonnaise
¼ cup chili sauce
¼ cup chopped green pepper
2 tablespoons sliced green onion
1 teaspoon lemon juice
¼ cup whipping cream

Combine all ingredients. Stir until smooth. Serve with Cioppino Salad.

Yield: 6 to 8 servings

Exotic Chicken Salad

4 cups cooked chicken
1 cup chopped celery
2 cups seedless grapes
    OR 1 cup water chestnuts
1 cup pineapple (fresh is good)
1 cup slivered almonds
Shredded coconut
1½ cups mayonnaise
1 teaspoon curry powder
1 tablespoon lemon juice

Combine mayonnaise, curry, and lemon juice; add remaining ingredients and mix well to combine. Chill several hours. Garnish with coconut and additional almonds.

Yield: 8 servings

CURRIED CHICKEN SALAD WITH GRAPES AND ALMONDS

4 chicken breast halves
Water
Several celery ribs
Instant chicken bouillon, to taste
Onion flakes, to taste
1 cup seedless grapes
1 cup celery, sliced
⅓ cup sliced green onion, including green tops
Pineapple chunks, optional
Juice of ½ lemon
1 teaspoon curry powder, or to taste
½ cup or more mayonnaise, to taste
¼ cup slivered almonds

Simmer chicken breast halves in water to cover, to which you have added the celery ribs, bouillon, and onion flakes. Simmer about an hour or until chicken is done. Debone, if necessary, and dice. (You should have approximately 1 pound cooked, deboned meat.)

Place diced chicken in attractive bowl. Add the 1 cup celery, grapes, green onion (and pineapple, if desired). Mix together lightly. Add lemon juice, curry powder, and mayonnaise to taste. Mix well. Chill.

Just before serving, add slivered almonds. Garnish as desired with cantaloupe, grapes, or other fresh fruit.

Yield: 6 servings

CHINESE SALAD

1 head lettuce
2 cups boneless chicken (2 whole breasts), cooked
6 green onions, tops included
2 tablespoons toasted sesame seeds
½ package wontons cut in strips and fried until crisp
    and light in color
6 or 8 ribs of celery

Combine all ingredients. Toss with dressing just before serving.

Dressing

2 tablespoon sugar (3 packages sugar substitute)
2 teaspoons salt
1 teaspoon Accent
½ teaspoon pepper
4 tablespoons white vinegar
½ cup salad oil

Combine all ingredients several hours before serving.

FESTIVE HOLIDAY SALAD

2 packages (6 ounces each) lemon gelatin
3 cups water
1 cup pineapple juice
1½ cups small marshmallows
1 can (8¾ ounces) crushed pineapple
3 or 4 diced bananas

Set gelatin as directed on package until syrupy, using pineapple juice as part of liquid, then add marshmallows, pineapple, and bananas.

Topping
1 cup orange juice or pineapple juice
1 well beaten egg
¼ cup sugar
1 tablespoon cornstarch
½ pint whipping cream
shredded cheese

Mix sugar, cornstarch, and egg. Heat juice and thicken with cornstarch mixture. Cool. Whip cream and blend with sauce. Spread on gelatin and sprinkle with shredded cheese. For festive look, add cherries and nuts to cream mixture.

Yield: 15 servings

LAYERED HOLIDAY SALAD

1 package (3 ounces) lime gelatin
2 cups water or other liquid
1 package (3 ounces) lemon gelatin
1 cup crushed pineapple
½ pound miniature marshmallows
1 cup whipping cream
1 package (3 ounces) cream cheese, room temperature
½ cup mayonnaise
1 package (3 ounces) cherry gelatin
2 cups boiling water

Dissolve lime gelatin in 2 cups boiling water. Pour into bottom of oblong pan. Chill until set.

Drain juice from pineapple and add enough water to juice to make 2 cups. Heat liquid and pour over lemon gelatin, stirring until gelatin is dissolved. Stir in marshmallows while gelatin is hot. Cool mixture.

Whip cream and to it add softened cream cheese and mayonnaise. Sir in lemon gelatin along with drained pineapple. Pour this mixture over set lime gelatin. Chill until set.

Dissolve cherry gelatin in remaining 2 cups boiling water. Cool until syrupy. Pour very carefully over set lemon gelatin mixture, being careful not to displace any of the lemon gelatin mixture. Chill until firm.

Cut into squares to serve.

Yield: 10 to 12 servings

LEMON CLOUD SALAD

1 package (3 ounces) lemon gelatin
1 package (3 ounces) lime gelatin
1 can (15¼ ounces) crushed pineapple, drained, reserving juice
2 tablespoons horseradish
2 tablespoons lemon juice
1 can sweetened condensed milk
1 cup mayonnaise
1 cup chopped celery
1 large carton cottage cheese
1 cup chopped nuts (optional)

Dissolve gelatin in reserved pineapple juice and boiling water to make 2 cups. Add pineapple, horseradish, lemon juice, and condensed milk. Chill until thick and syrupy. Add mayonnaise, celery, cottage cheese, and nuts; stir to combine. Refrigerate until set.

Yield: 12 servings

SANTA CINNAMON SALAD

½ cup cinnamon candies
1 package (6 ounces) cherry gelatin
1 can (15¼ ounces) crushed pineapple and juice
2 cups diced apples
1 cup chopped walnuts

Dissolve cinnamon candies and gelatin in 2 cups boiling water. Add remaining ingredients and chill until set.

Note: Red food coloring can be added for a brighter holiday color.

Yield: 9 servings

ONE-CUP SALAD

1 package (3 ounces) lemon gelatin, dissolved in 1 cup
    boiling water, cooled
1 cup finely grated cabbage
1 cup coconut
1 cup chopped pecans
1 can (8 ounces) crushed pineapple
1 cup finely chopped celery
1 cup mayonnaise
1 package Dream Whip, prepared according to directions

Combine all ingredients and chill to set. Can be prepared
in a mold.

Yield: 6 servings

RAINBOW SALAD (KID'S DELIGHT)

1 package (3-ounces) each blackberry, lime, lemon,
    orange, and strawberry gelatin
1 large carton sour cream

Beginning with blackberry gelatin, dissolve gelatin in
one cup boiling water. Divide in half. To one half, add 3 tablespoons cold water. Chill in 9x9 pan (8x8 isn't large enough).
After it has set, add ⅓ cup sour cream to second half of gelatin,
beating with egg beater until smooth. Pour on chilled gelatin.
Let set. Continue this process until all five flavors have been
used.

Yield: 9 to 12 servings

Raspberry Salad

    1 package (6 ounces) raspberry gelatin
    1¼ cup hot water
    1 package (10 ounces) frozen raspberries and juice
    1 cup crushed pineapple, drained
    2 bananas, diced
    1 cup nuts, chopped

Combine gelatin and hot water and mix until dissolved. Add remaining ingredients and refrigerate until firm.

Yield: 9 servings

Red, White, and Blue Salad

    2 packages (3 ounces each) raspberry gelatin
    2 cups hot water
    1 package (10 ounces) frozen raspberries (thawed)
    1 cup half and half
    ½ cup sugar
    1 envelope unflavored gelatin
    ¼ cup cold water
    1 cup sour cream
    1 teaspoon vanilla
    1 can (16 ounces) blueberries (undrained)

Dissolve 1 package raspberry gelatin in 1 cup hot water. Stir in raspberries. Pour into 8-cup mold. Refrigerate until firm. Heat half and half mixed with sugar. Soften unflavored gelatin in cold water. Stir into warm cream mixture until gelatin dissolves. Remove from heat and stir in sour cream and vanilla. Cool mixture; pour over first layer and refrigerate until firm. Dissolve 1 package raspberry gelatin in 1 cup hot water. Add blueberries and juice, stirring to combine. Cool mixture and pour over second layer. Chill until firm.

Note: This recipe can be doubled and made in an oblong pan.

BLUEBERRY DELIGHT

1 package (6 ounces) raspberry gelatin
2 cups boiling water
1 package (3 ounces) cream cheese, softened
½ pint whipping cream, whipped
1 can (15¾ ounces) crushed pineapple plus juice
1 can blueberries plus juice

Dissolve gelatin in boiling water. Beat cream cheese for one minute. Add pineapple, blueberries, and whipped cream. Pour into mold. May be garnished with whipped cream and banana slices.

Yield: 8 servings

LIME SALAD

1 package (3 ounces) lime gelatin
1 cup pear juice, heated
1 package (3 ounces) cream cheese
5 pear halves, pureed
1 cup whipping cream, whipped
Slivered almonds
Maraschino cherries

Dissolve gelatin in hot pear juice. Combine cream cheese and gelatin in a blender container and blend until smooth. Set until syrupy. Add pears and whipped cream to gelatin mixture and refrigerate until set. Garnish with almonds and cherries.

Yield: 9 servings

SURPRISE SALAD

2 cups pretzels, crushed
3 tablespoons sugar
¾ cup butter, melted
1 package (8 ounces) cream cheese
1 cup sugar
1 carton (12 ounces) nondairy whipped topping
1 can (8¼ ounces) crushed pineapple, well drained
1 package (6 ounces) raspberry gelatin
3 cups boiling water
1 package frozen raspberries

Mix pretzels, sugar, and butter. Press into an oblong pan. Bake at 400 degrees for 5 minutes. Cool.

Mix cream cheese, sugar, and whipped topping. Fold in pineapple. Spread mixture on crust. Dissolve gelatin in boiling water. Add frozen raspberries. Let set until syrupy. Pour over cream cheese mixture and refrigerate until set. Garnish with whipped topping and crushed pretzels. Serve on individual plates on lettuce leaves.

Yield: 18 servings

CRANBERRY GELATIN MOLD

2 packages (3 ounces each) red gelatin (cherry or raspberry) dissolved in
2 cups boiling water
2 cups raw cranberries
2 red apples, unpeeled
½ cup sugar
2 cups chopped celery
1 cup chopped nuts
1 can (15¼ ounces) pineapple tidbits, drained
1 package frozen raspberries, thawed

Refrigerate gelatin. Grind cranberries and apples, sprinkle
with sugar, and let stand. When gelatin starts to set, add remaining ingredients.

FLUFFY PINK SALAD

1 carton (8 ounces) frozen whipped topping, thawed
1 can sweetened condensed milk
1 can cherry pie filling
2 cups miniature marshmallows
1 can tropical fruit, drained
1 can mandarin oranges, drained

Beat milk into the whipped topping. Fold in cherry pie
filling. Blend well. Add marshmallows, tropical fruit, and mandarin oranges. Mix well.

Refrigerator 8 hours or overnight.

Serve on a lettuce leaf.

Yield: 8 servings

FROZEN PINEAPPLE SALAD

1 pint sour cream
2 tablespoons lemon juice
½ cup sugar (scant)
⅛ teaspoon salt
1 can (8 ounces) crushed pineapple (well drained)
¾ cup chopped maraschino cherries
¼ cup pecans (optional)
1 banana, diced
⅓ cup maraschino cherry juice

Mix sour cream, lemon juice, sugar, and salt. Add remaining ingredients and mix well. Pour mixture into muffin tins lined with cup cake papers and freeze until firm. Unmold to serve. Can be frozen in a small ring mold.

Yield: 10 servings

NELDA'S ORANGE GELATIN RING

2 packages (3 ounces each) orange-flavored gelatin
2 cups boiling liquid (water or fruit juice)
1 pint orange sherbet
1 can (11 ounces) mandarin oranges, drained

Dissolve gelatin in boiling liquid. Immediately add orange sherbet and stir until melted. Add oranges. Pour into 1½ quart ring mold and chill until firm. Unmold and fill center with Fabulous Five Salad (p. 180).

REUNION SALAD

1 tablespoon flour
½ cup granulated sugar
1¼ teaspoon salt, divided
1¼ cups pineapple juice (from drained pineapple)
1 egg, beaten
1 teaspoon lemon juice
½ box Acini de pepe pasta
1 tablespoon salad oil
1 can (15¼ ounces) pineapple chunks, cut in half,
    drained, reserving juice
1 large can mandarin oranges
1 can (15¼ ounces) crushed pineapple, drained, reserv-
    ing juice
1 can (16 ounces) fruit cocktail, drained
1 carton (8 ounces) frozen whipped topping, thawed

Combine flour, sugar, and ¼ teaspoon salt. Stir in juice
and eggs and cook until thick. Add lemon juice and cool. (Can
be set in pan of ice water to hurry it up.) Cook Acini de pepe
pasta in 6 cups of boiling water with 1 teaspoon salt. Cook for
8 minutes or until tender. Add oil and drain. Rinse and cool.
Add thick juice and all the fruit. Chill overnight. Just before
serving, fold in the whipped topping (or add it an hour or two
ahead, but it thickens on standing).

FABULOUS FIVE SALAD

> 2 cans (11 ounces each) mandarin oranges, drained
> 2 cans (13 ounces each) pineapple chunks, drained
> 1 cup flaked coconut
> 1½ cups commercial sour cream
>   OR 1 cup whipping cream, whipped
> 2 cups cut-up or miniature marshmallows
> Red grapes could also be added for color

Mix all ingredients. Chill several hours or overnight. Serve on a lettuce leaf or mound into center of Nelda's Orange Gelatin Ring (p. 178).

Yield: 12 to 15 servings

WALDORF SALAD

> 3 to 4 apples, diced
> 1 cup sliced celery
> ½ cup chopped walnuts
> ½ cup mayonnaise or salad dressing
> 1 tablespoon sugar
> 1 tablespoon canned milk
> 1 teaspoon grated lemon rind
> 2 tablespoons lemon juice

Place apples, celery, and walnuts in a bowl. Combine rest of ingredients in another bowl and mix well. Add to fruit mixture and toss to combine.

Variation: 1 cup pineapple tidbits can be added.

Yield: 4 servings

KITTY'S FRUIT COMPOTE

3 grapefruit
6 oranges
1 pound seedless grapes
3 large apples (Granny Smith are good)
3 bananas
1 can (16 ounces) crushed pineapple (unsweetened)
1 can (16 ounces) fruit cocktail or any fruit in season
1 can (6 ounces) frozen orange juice concentrate

Peel and section membrane from grapefruit and oranges. Leave peelings on apples and dice. Add the rest of the ingredients and mix well. Store in an air-tight container in the refrigerator. Will keep for one week.

Yield: 25 servings

FRUIT SALAD

1 cup peaches
1 cup pears
1 cup Royal Ann cherries
1 cup pineapple
1 package (one pound) marshmallows, cut up
1 pint whipping cream, whipped
Tokay grapes as desired
1 banana diced

Drain fruit and cut into bite-sized pieces. Mix all ingredients together and let stand overnight. Add bananas just before serving. Add blanched almonds if desired.

Yield: 6 servings

SNOW-TIME SURPRISE

This is a hot garnish salad. Serve it on the salad plate or meat platter.

Fill peach half with crushed pineapple, drizzle some French dressing over the top, and broil for about 10 minutes. Serve broiled peach at once on a galax leaf or parsley, with stuffed olives.

Salad Dressings

CELERY-SEED DRESSING

⅓ cup sugar
1 teaspoon salt
1 teaspoon dry mustard
1 teaspoon grated onion
¼ cup vinegar
1 cup salad oil
1 teaspoon celery seed

Mix dry ingredients; add onion and vinegar. Add oil, 1 tablespoon at a time, beating constantly with electric beater. Stir in celery seed.

Yield: 1½ cups

MARSHMALLOW DRESSING

1 cup marshmallow creme
¼ cup salad dressing or mayonnaise
1½ teaspoons grated orange peel
2 teaspoons orange juice
1 to 2 teaspoons lemon juice, fresh, or frozen

Blend all ingredients together until well mixed. Serve over fruit salad.

Yield: 1 cup

HOTEL UTAH THOUSAND ISLAND DRESSING

1 quart salad dressing (Miracle Whip)
5 hard boiled eggs, finely chopped
½ cup finely chopped celery
1½ tablespoons minced onion
1 bottle chili sauce
2 tablespoons sweet pickle relish
Sugar to taste

Combine all ingredients and refrigerate for several hours to combine flavors.

FRUIT SALAD DRESSING

½ cup sugar
2½ tablespoons cornstarch
⅔ cup boiling water
Juice of 1 medium orange
Juice of ½ lemon
    OR 2 tablespoons pineapple juice
1 cup whipping cream, whipped

Combine sugar, cornstarch, and boiling water in a saucepan. Cook on low temperature until thickened. Cook 5 minutes. Remove from heat and add juices; refrigerate. When ready to serve add whipped cream.

.

August

Refreshing Antidotes

Imagination is more important than knowledge.

Albert Einstein

Man loves company even if it is only
That of a small burning candle.

Georg Christoph Lichtenberg

Houseguests

As summer reunions are planned, visits from out-of-town family members are eagerly anticipated. Pamper those long-awaited house guests with the comforts of home, anticipating their every need. Before they arrive spruce up the guest room. Make sure there is a clock radio in the room. Leave a selection of the latest magazines. Supply a luggage holder, hangers, and an extra robe and slippers. Place a bouquet of fresh flowers by the bed. In the bathroom have a basket filled with bubble bath, scented soap, loofa sponge, lotion, and an extra toothbrush and toothpaste. Turn down the bed at night and leave a sweet surprise on the pillow. A carafe filled with ice water and a glass is a welcomed gesture. Let your guests sleep in late and indulge them with breakfast in bed. Supply them with warm, fluffy towels for their morning shower. After their stay has come to an end, send them home with a tin of your special cookies.

Family Reunion

Saurbraten (p. 247) or

Trimmed Brisket (p. 249)

Garden Potato Salad (p. 163)

Picnic Rice Salad (p. 165)

Spinach Salad (p. 159) or

Sheila's Broccoli Salad (p. 161)

Kitty's Fruit Compote (p. 181)

Oatmeal Cake (p. 113)

Turtle Bars (p. 273)

Pineapple Shrub (p. 198) or

Strawberry Crush (p. 201)

Fun Tips

Any beverage, even water, can be perked up by using special ice cubes, molds, or rings.

* Color the water for ice cubes with food coloring before freezing.

* Freeze mint leaves, flowers, maraschino cherries, citrus peels, or gum drops in ice cubes or ice molds. Fill the container halfway with water and freeze. Arrange the decorations on the ice, carefully add ½ inch of water and refreeze. When the decoration is set, fill the container the rest of the way and freeze thoroughly.

* If serving punch, make ice cubes or rings using the punch so the drink won't be diluted.

* Make "fruit cubes" by cutting peaches, strawberries, pineapple, or watermelon into pieces, dipping them in lemon juice and freezing them separately on cookie sheet.

* Frost glasses by putting them wet into the freezer one hour before serving time.

* Dip the rim of a glass in water and then in sugar for a fruit drink or salt for a vegetable drink. Let it sit to firm the coating.

* Place a scoop of vanilla ice cream in hot chocolate for a special treat.

Family Reunions

* Collect family favorite recipes and compile in a cookbook to pass out at the reunion.

* Sponge paint T-shirts—everyone the same or each individual family do theirs alike.

* Have a theme party—use a country as a theme and

decorate and plan food around it.

* Play Bingo; use white elephants or draw for prizes—include a few draws as tickets to help clean up.
* Bury a treasure—put a letter or possession in a box, bury it, mark where it is, and open it next year.

Other

* Throw an old-fashioned ice cream social where everyone brings their favorite ice cream. Supply the toppings, spoons, and bowls.
* Plan a "you are special day" for each of your children or grandchildren.
* Roast hot dogs (over a fire in the barbecue) and tell spooky stories.
* Have a "Back to School" Party for parents ("I am free again"). Give everyone a handkerchief to wave goodbye to those school children.

Refreshing Antidotes

Beverages

ESKIMO PUNCH

1 can (6 ounces) frozen lemonade concentrate
1 can (6 ounces) frozen grape juice concentrate
Lemon–lime carbonated beverage, as desired
Ice

Mix lemonade and grape juice according to instructions on can. Mix equal portions lemonade and grape juice together in punch bowl or pitcher. Add carbonated beverage and ice, as desired.

CRANBERRY TODDY

¾ cup brown sugar
1 cup water
¾ teaspoon cloves
½ teaspoon cinnamon
½ teaspoon allspice
¼ teaspoon nutmeg
¼ teaspoon salt
4 cups unsweetened pineapple juice
3 cups water
2 cans (1-pound each) jellied cranberry sauce
Red food coloring (optional)
Lemon slices

In saucepan combine brown sugar, 1 cup water, spices, and salt. Bring to boiling. Add pineapple juice and 3 cups water. Crush cranberry sauce and add to spice mixture. Heat thoroughly; add food coloring and serve with lemon slices.

ROSY RASPBERRY PUNCH

3 cups unsweetened pineapple juice
1 package (10 ounces) frozen raspberries, partially thawed
1 pint vanilla ice cream
1 pint raspberry sherbet
2 cups carbonated water
Pineapple chunks, for garnish (optional)
Maraschino cherries, for garnish (optional)

In blender container, combine pineapple juice and raspberries. Cover. Blend till smooth; strain. Pour into large mixer bowl; add ice cream and sherbet. Beat till smooth. Pour into punch bowl. Slowly pour in soda, stirring with up-and-down motion. Serve immediately. Garnish each serving with a pineapple chunk and maraschino cherry speared on a cocktail stick.

Yield: 9½ cups

TOM'S PUNCH

6 cups cold water
3½ cups sugar
1 can (12 ounces) frozen orange juice concentrate
4 cans water
1 can (6 ounces) frozen lemon juice
    OR juice of 6 lemons
1 can (46 ounces) unsweetened pineapple juice
6 large or 8 medium bananas, mashed
½ teaspoon coconut extract
3 quarts ginger ale

Boil 6 cups water and sugar 3 minutes. Cool. Add orange juice and 4 cans water, lemon, and pineapple and blend. Add coconut extract. Freeze in ½ gallon milk cartons. Leave head room for expansion.

Remove cartons from freezer 3 to 4 hours before needed. Add ginger ale. Serve slushy.

Note: An ice ring frozen with lemon and orange slices and chopped cherries may be used.

Yield: 60 punch-cup servings

TOMATO JUICE CRAB COCKTAIL

1 can crab
1 can (16 ounces) grapefruit (not drained)
1 pint catsup
1 can (46 ounces) tomato juice
2 or 3 lemons, juiced
Salt, sugar, and Worcestershire sauce to taste

Combine all ingredients and chill.

FRUIT COMPOTE

1 gallon crushed unsweetened pineapple
9 packages frozen strawberries
    OR 2 quarts fresh strawberries
7 bananas, sliced
1 can (12 ounces) frozen lemonade concentrate

Combine pineapple, lemonade, and strawberries and refrigerate at least 1 hour. When ready to serve add bananas. Serve in a cup with a spoon.

Yield: 36 servings

TOMATO BOUILLON

1 can (46 ounces) tomato juice
2 beef bouillon cubes
Salt to taste
Dash pepper
Whipped cream
1 teaspoon chopped parsley

Heat juice and bouillon cubes until boiling. Season with salt and pepper to taste.
Place 1 teaspoon whipped cream on each serving and sprinkle with chopped parsley.

WITCHES' BREW

1 quart cranberry juice, chilled
2 pints lime sherbet

Fill punch cups with cranberry juice and add a heaping spoonful of sherbet.

Yield: 12 small cups

PINK LADY COCKTAIL

1 bottle (16 ounces) cranberry juice cocktail
1 can (12 ounces) pineapple juice
1 can (18 ounces) grapefruit juice

Combine juices, chill. Serve over ice.

Yield: 8 to 10 servings

INDIAN SUMMER SIPPER

1 can (12 ounces) frozen orange juice concentrate, thawed
1 can (12 ounces) frozen lemonade concentrate, thawed
10 cups water
2 cups sugar
1 teaspoon almond extract

Mix all ingredients together. Can be served hot or cold.

Yield: 30 servings

BLUSHING LEMONADE

1 can (6 ounces) frozen pink lemonade concentrate
1 package (10 ounces) frozen strawberries
1 can (13 ounces) crushed pineapple with juice
2 bottles (16 ounces each) ginger ale

Partially thaw strawberries and lemonade concentrate. In blender jar, combine strawberries, pineapple, and lemonade. Blend until smooth. Chill. Just before serving, stir in chilled ginger ale. Pour over ice.

Yield: 8 servings

FRUIT FREEZE

1 pint sherbet (lemon, lime, or orange)
1 quart ginger ale

In a punch bowl, soften sherbet with a potato masher; gradually add ginger ale, and mix to combine.

GRAPEFRUIT SLUSH

3 cans unsweetened grapefruit
Juice of 3 lemons
1½ cups sugar
1 small bottle maraschino cherries, cut in half (reserve liquid)
3 bottles (16 ounces each) lemon–lime carbonated beverage

Combine grapefruit and lemon juice and beat until grapefruit is broken. Add sugar, cherries, and juice. Freeze until slushy. Just before serving, add lemon–lime carbonated beverage.

MINT HOT CHOCOLATE MALT MIX

2 cups chocolate-flavored malted milk powder
1 cup white butter mints
3 cups nonfat dry milk powder
2 cups presweetened cocoa mix

In blender container, combine 1 cup of the malted milk powder and the mints. Cover and blend 1 minute or until mints are finely chopped. Turn into mixing bowl. Add remaining malted milk powder, and cocoa mix. Stir well. Store in an airtight container.

Yield: 7 cups mix

For 1 serving: Stir ¼ cup mix into ¾ cup boiling water. Top with a marshmallow.

HOT TOMATO DRINK

1 can (46 ounces) tomato juice
1 can (6 ounces) frozen orange juice concentrate
2 teaspoons lime juice
1 lemon, juiced

Combine all ingredients; heat thoroughly and serve hot.

Yield: 6 to 8 servings

MINTED LEMONADE

1 can (12 ounces) frozen lemonade concentrate
Several stems of mint
1 can (12 ounces) lemon-lime carbonated beverage

Dilute lemonade using 2½ cans of water. Add mint to lemonade and let stand for 1 to 2 hours or until desired mint flavor is reached. Remove mint. Add carbonated beverage before serving.

Yield: 6 servings

PINEAPPLE SHRUB

2 cans (46 ounces each) pineapple juice
Juice of 8 lemons
Juice of 8 oranges
Juice of 3 limes
2 cups sugar
1 cup mint leaves (optional)
4 quarts ginger ale
2 quarts carbonated water
1 pint fresh strawberries, washed, hulled, and sliced

Combine all juices, sugar, and mint leaves and chill thoroughly. Just before serving add remaining ingredients. Pour over ice and garnish with thin slices of lemon, orange, or lime.

Yield 35 to 40 servings

Yulenog

2 quarts dairy eggnog
1 quart whole milk
Rum flavoring to taste
1 pint whipping cream, stiffly beaten

Combine eggnog, milk, and rum flavoring. Fold in whipped cream. Chill at least 3 hours.

Yield: 24 servings

Wassail

1 cup sugar
4 cups water
2 cinnamon sticks
8 allspice berries
10 whole cloves
1 piece ginger
1 can (6 ounces) frozen orange juice concentrate
1 can (6 ounces) frozen lemonade concentrate
2 quarts apple cider

Combine sugar and water and simmer for 5 minutes. Place all spices in a cheesecloth bag; add to sugar water and let steep for one hour. Remove spice bag just before serving, add juices; heat and serve immediately.

MELONADE

2 cups watermelon, cubed
1 pint fresh or 2 cups frozen, whole strawberries
½ cup sugar
⅓ cup lemon juice
2 cups ice cubes
Mint leaves, watermelon cubes, and whole berries for
    garnish (optional)

Clean and hull fresh strawberries. Place fruits, sugar, and lemon juice in blender. Blend well. Gradually add ice, blending until smooth. Garnish as desired. Serve immediately.

Yield: About 5 cups

MOCK SANGRIA

1½ cups boiling water
1 teaspoon dried mint leaves
½ cup honey
1 cup orange juice
1 cup grape juice
¾ cup lemon juice
2 cups chilled water or carbonated water
Lemon or orange slices (optional)

Combine boiling water and mint leaves; let stand 5 minutes; strain. Stir in the honey, orange juice, grape juice, and lemon juice. Cover and chill. When serving, stir in the chilled water. Garnish with fruit slices.

Yield: 8 servings

Mock Mint Julep

1 jar (10 ounces) mint-flavored apple jelly
1½ cups water
1 quart club soda or seltzer
Lime slices or mint sprigs
Maraschino cherries
Crushed ice

Combine jelly and water in saucepan and heat until jelly melts. Refrigerate. Fill glasses with crushed ice. Pour glasses half-full with syrup and remainder with club soda or seltzer. Garnish with lime slices or mint sprigs and maraschino cherries.

Yield: 6 to 8 servings

Strawberry Crush

2 packages unsweetened strawberry flavored drink mix
3½ cups sugar
2 cans (6 ounces each) frozen pink lemonade concentrate
1 gallon water
2 packages (10 ounces each) frozen strawberries, pureed

Combine all ingredients and serve over ice.

Yield: 1½ gallons

SUNRISE FRAPPE FRUIT CUP

½ cup sugar
1 can (6 ounces) frozen orange juice concentrate
1 can (6 ounces) frozen pink lemonade concentrate
1 package (10 ounces) frozen sliced strawberries
1 package (10 ounces) frozen raspberries
1 can (20 ounces) crushed pineapple
1 banana, cubed
1 can (12 ounces) ginger ale
Orange twists for garnish (optional)

Thaw all frozen ingredients. In oblong glass pan, combine all ingredients except ginger ale. Mix well. Add ginger ale. Cover and freeze about 4 hours or until slush consistency. Serve in individual dishes. Garnish with orange twist.

Yield: 14 servings

HELEN'S PUNCH

5 pounds sugar
1 quart pineapple juice
1 pint grapefruit juice
1 pint orange juice
6 ounces lemon juice (not lemonade)
    OR juice of 6 lemons
1 ounce citric acid
5 bananas, mashed,
    OR 3 packages frozen strawberries

Combine all ingredients and add enough water to make five gallons. Freeze until slushy.
For a smooth slush, whirl frozen juice mixture in blender.

Yield: 5 gallons

CIDER–CITRUS PUNCH

1 gallon (16 cups) apple cider or apple juice
1 can (6 ounces) frozen lemonade concentrate
1 can (6 ounces) frozen orange juice concentrate
½ cup packed brown sugar
1 tablespoon whole cloves
1 tablespoon whole allspice

In large kettle, combine the cider or apple juice, undiluted concentrates, and the brown sugar. Stir until concentrates thaw and sugar dissolves. Tie cloves and allspice in cheesecloth bag; add to cider. Cover and simmer 20 minutes, stirring occasionally. Remove spice bag and discard. Serve punch hot.

For a festive flair, garnish the individual drinks with cocktail picks speared with fresh cranberries and an accordion strip of lemon peel.

Yield: 18 cups of punch

HOMEMADE ROOTBEER

1 teaspoon yeast dissolved in ½ cup warm water
2 cups sugar
2 tablespoons rootbeer extract

Combine all ingredients and place in a gallon jar. Fill the rest of the jar with luke-warm water; put a lid on it and let it stand at room temperature for 12 hours. Refrigerate until well chilled.

TROPICAL SLUSH

4 cans (46 ounces each) pineapple-grapefruit juice
5 bottles (16 ounces each) lemon-lime carbonated beverage
Green or red food coloring
Orange or lemon slices

Remove tops of juice cans and freeze contents in the cans. Remove from freezer one hour before serving.

When ready to serve, transfer frozen juice to punch bowl and add carbonated beverage. Add red food coloring and garnish with citrus slices.

LESLIE'S FROZEN SLUSH

6 cups water
4 cups sugar
1 can (46 ounces) pineapple juice
1 can (6 ounces) frozen orange juice concentrate
2 lemons, juiced
7 bananas, mashed
2 packages frozen strawberries or raspberries
1½ cups frozen blueberries
Ginger ale or 7-Up as desired (about one quart)

Boil water and sugar until clear, about 5 minutes; add juices and fruit. Freeze 24 hours. Remove from freezer one hour before serving.

Before serving add ginger ale or 7-Up to taste.

Yield: 20 servings

September

Harvest Companions

*Show me your garden and
I shall show you who you are.*

A. Austin

Buffets

A buffet is a simple way to feed a crowd and can showcase your creativity. The table linens will vary the effect you want to attain dramatically. An old quilt, a rug, a white linen cloth, colored cloths, a woven cloth and table runner, or a metallic cloth will define the theme. What to do with the silverware? Wrap them in napkins and stand them in a glass bowl or basket, or tie them with ribbon, tuck in a small flower and arrange on the table. Plates can be stacked with a colorful napkin peeking out between each plate. Use a variety of serving pieces: silver, china, pottery, crystal, and baskets. Remember, serve foods that are easy to handle and eat.

Fun Tips

Choosing fruits and vegetables is a matter of experience and "touch." Citrus fruits should feel heavy for the size (the heavier, the juicier). Peaches, plums, pears, avocados, and tomatoes should give slightly, under a little pressure. Melons, pineapples, and squash should sound like a thump on your wrist. The flower end of melons and the stem end of pineapples should smell sweet.

Squeeze a fresh lemon over cooked vegetables before you toss them with butter.

Harvest Hobo Party

Garden Vegetable Stew (p. 18) or

Vegetable Stroganoff (p. 17)

Malted Breadsticks (p. 82)

Georgia Peach Pie (p. 120)

Cinnamon Ice Cream (p. 108)

Mock Sangria (p. 200)

Harvest Hobo Party

* For a unique meal, serve stone soup—each guest brings a vegetable cleaned and ready for the soup pot. Cook vegetables in a small pan and add to the stock. Serve in soup cans.

* Organize a scavenger hunt or a treasure hunt while the soup or stew is cooking. The "treasure" could be dessert, a movie, game, or entertainment.

* While eating dessert, gather around a hobo fire (charcoal in a wheelbarrow).

Labor Day

* Draw jobs out of a jar and form a family specialty crew to complete house and garden chores. Then visit an antique store or garage sale and look for old books, tools, or whatever interests you.

* Plan a puppet show—have the children make puppets from lunch bags (put the flap in front so the child's hand can move the face).

Harvest Companions

Vegetables and Side Dishes

WILD RICE EXCELLENTE

2½ cups chicken broth
½ cup wild rice (rinsed)
¼ cup butter
1 small onion, finely chopped
1 cup sliced fresh mushrooms
½ cup finely chopped celery
¼ cup finely chopped green pepper
1 can (5 ounces) water chestnuts, chopped
1 cup long-grain white rice
1 teaspoon poultry seasoning
½ teaspoon salt
Dash pepper
2 tablespoons snipped parsley

Combine chicken broth and wild rice in covered saucepan; bring to a boil. Reduce heat; simmer for 20 minutes. Meanwhile, melt butter in skillet; sauté onion, mushrooms, celery, green pepper, and water chestnuts. When wild rice has simmered 20 minutes, add sautéed vegetables, long-grain white rice, poultry seasoning, salt, and pepper. Simmer, covered for 20 additional minutes. Stir in snipped parsley.

Yield: 6 to 8 servings

ZUCCHINI CASSEROLE

6 slices bacon
1 onion, chopped
1 can (10¾ ounces) cream of mushroom soup or cream
    of celery soup
⅓ cup milk
3 to 4 small zucchini, sliced
2 tomatoes, sliced
2 cups shredded cheddar cheese

Fry bacon until crisp, then crumble; sauté onions in bacon grease; drain. Combine bacon, onions, soup, and milk. In a casserole, layer zucchini, tomato, then soup, 1 cup cheese, and then layer again ending with cheese. Bake at 300 degrees for 30 minutes or until cheese is melted.

BAKED BEANS

1 can each: garbanzo beans, drained
                   lima beans, drained
                   kidney beans, drained
                   pork and beans
                   baked beans
½ pound ground beef, browned and drained
1 onion, chopped, cooked with ground beef
5 slices bacon, cooked
1 cup brown sugar
½ cup vinegar
½ cup ketchup
Salt to taste

Combine all ingredients and bake covered at 350 degrees for 1 hour

California Bake

1 package (10 ounces) frozen cauliflower
1 package (10 ounces) frozen broccoli
2 tablespoons butter or margarine
½ teaspoon flour
¼ teaspoon salt
¼ teaspoon pepper
1½ cups hot milk
¼ cup chopped onion
1 can (8 ounces) water chestnuts, sliced (optional)
¾ cup grated Cheddar cheese
10 soda crackers, crushed
2 tablespoons melted butter (to moisten soda crackers)

Cook vegetables according to package directions; drain. Place vegetables in a 2 quart casserole; add water chestnuts, if desired. Melt 2 tablespoons of butter, add flour, salt, and pepper and stir well. Stir in milk and bring to a boil. Sprinkle onion and cheese over vegetables and pour sauce over all. Mix soda crackers and 2 tablespoons melted butter to moisten; sprinkle over casserole. Bake, uncovered, at 350 degrees for 45 minutes.

Yield: 6 to 8 servings

ARTICHOKE CASSEROLE

4 cups medium white sauce
4 teaspoons chicken bouillon granules
2 cans artichoke hearts, drained well
¾ cup grated Swiss cheese
½ cup saltine cracker crumbs
½ cup bread crumbs
2 tablespoons butter, melted
1 tablespoon Parmesan cheese

Combine white sauce, bouillon, artichoke hearts, and Swiss cheese. Place in a casserole and bake at 300 degrees for 20 minutes. Mix cracker crumbs, butter, and Parmesan cheese and sprinkle over casserole. Continue cooking until crumbs are toasted.

CHEESY SPINACH BAKE

1 can (15 ounces) spinach
4 eggs, beaten
1 cup milk
1 cup shredded Swiss cheese
1 cup cubed firm white bread
½ cup sliced green onions
¼ cup grated Parmesan cheese

Drain spinach squeezing out excess liquid. Combine all ingredients; pour into 1 quart baking dish. Cover and bake at 375 degrees 25 to 30 minutes or until tests done.

Yield: 6 servings

SEPTEMBER RICE PILAF

¾ cup blanched slivered almonds
¼ cup butter, melted
1½ cups long grain rice (Uncle Ben's)
3 cups water
3 chicken bouillon cubes
Dash salt
Dash pepper
Parsley for garnish

Sauté almonds in butter over medium heat until lightly browned. Remove almonds and add rice to pan. Sauté rice stirring continually, until lightly browned. Add water, bouillon cubes, salt, and pepper to rice. Spoon into buttered covered casserole. Bake covered at 350 degrees for 30 minutes; remove lid and continue baking for 10 more minutes. Add almonds. Garnish with parsley.

Yield: 8 to 10 servings

Note: Pine nuts could be substituted for the almonds.

VELDA'S RICE

3 cups cooked rice
2 cups grated sharp Cheddar cheese
½ cup (1 cube) butter, melted
2 eggs, beaten
1½ cups milk
1 green pepper, diced
1 onion, diced
Salt to taste

Combine all ingredients and bake at 325 degrees for 45 minutes to 1 hour.

MAURINE'S ONIONS

12 medium-sized yellow onions, peeled and quartered
1 can (10¾ ounces) cream of mushroom soup
½ cup milk
1 jar (8 ounces) Cheese Whiz
1 cup crushed potato chips

Cook onions until tender. Drain in plastic colander very well. Combine soup, milk, and cheese. In a casserole, layer onions and cheese mixture. Bake at 275 degrees for 45 minutes. Sprinkle with potato chips and continue baking for another 15 minutes.

Yield: 8 to 10 servings

GLAZED CARROTS

12 small carrots, whole
2 tablespoons butter
⅓ cup honey
1 tablespoon lemon juice
½ cup crushed pineapple

Cook carrots until tender. In a frying pan, combine butter, honey, lemon juice, and pineapple. Add carrots and cook slowly on a low heat, turning frequently, until heated and glazed.

BAKED STUFFED TOMATOES

¼ cup chopped onion
¼ cup minced green pepper
1 tablespoon butter or margarine
1 cup mexicale corn
1 egg, slightly beaten
¼ teaspoon celery salt
¼ teaspoon marjoram
¼ teaspoon thyme
Dash salt
Dash pepper
6 medium tomatoes, cut in half

Sauté onion and green pepper in butter. Combine all ingredients except tomatoes and mix well. Stuff tomatoes with mixture. Bake at 400 degrees for 30 minutes.

CORN PUDDING

1 can creamed corn
2 cups milk
3 eggs, well beaten
1 cup cracker crumbs
½ cup chopped onion
½ cup diced pimento
2 teaspoons salt
Dash pepper
Green pepper rings

Heat corn and milk to simmering. Add crumbs, onion, pimento, and seasonings to eggs; stir in corn mixture. Pour into greased oblong pan. Top with pepper rings. Bake at 375 degrees about 40 to 45 minutes.

Yield: 8 servings

FIVE MINUTE CABBAGE

1 cup milk
2 cups shredded cabbage
¾ tablespoon flour
1 tablespoon melted butter or margarine
½ cup half and half
1 teaspoon salt
¼ teaspoon accent
Dash of pepper

Heat milk and add cabbage. Simmer 2 minutes, uncovered. Mix flour with butter. Add a little hot milk to flour mixture; stir into cabbage and cook 3 to 4 minutes, stirring constantly. Add half and half and seasonings. Heat thoroughly.

Yield: 4 servings

ASPARAGUS-BEAN CASSEROLE

1 can (16 ounces) French-style green beans
1 can (14½ ounces) asparagus
2 cans (10¾ ounces each) cream of mushroom soup
2 cups grated sharp Cheddar cheese, divided
1 cup crushed corn flakes

In a deep casserole, alternate layers of beans and asparagus. Pour soup over vegetables; sprinkle with 1 cup cheese, corn flakes then remaining 1 cup of cheese. Bake at 350 degrees for 1 hour.

STIR-FRY ZUCCHINI

    1 tablespoon vegetable oil
    4 cups zucchini, cut into 1½ inch strips
    1 cup onion, cut in wedges and separated
    1 tablespoon sesame seeds
    2 teaspoons soy sauce
    ⅛ teaspoon salt
    ½ teaspoon sesame oil (optional)

Heat vegetable oil in large skillet over medium heat. Add zucchini and onion. Stir-fry about 5 to 8 minutes. Sprinkle with sesame seeds, soy sauce, and sesame seed oil. Stir until blended.

    Yield: 4 servings

VEGETABLE COMBO

    1 head cauliflower, cut into flowerettes
    2 carrots, sliced in ¼-inch slices
    2 zucchini, sliced in ¼-inch slices
    2 yellow squash, sliced in ¼-inch slices
    1 teaspoon Italian salad dressing mix, unprepared
    Parmesan cheese

Place cauliflowerettes and sliced carrots on the bottom of a 2 quart casserole. Place zucchini and yellow squash on top. Cover tightly and microcook on high 6 minutes.

    Sprinkle Italian salad dressing and Parmesan cheese over all vegetables; cover. Microcook high 3 to 4 minutes or until vegetables are tender.

    Yield: 4 to 6 servings

LEMON CASHEW ASPARAGUS

1 package (10 ounces) frozen asparagus
    OR 1 pound fresh, cooked
¼ cup melted butter
Juice of one lemon
¼ cup cashew pieces

Arrange cooked asparagus on serving platter. Combine butter and lemon juice and pour over asparagus. Sprinkle with cashews.

Yield: 6 servings

POTATO CASSEROLE

1 bag (32 ounces) frozen hash brown potatoes, thawed
    OR 12 large potatoes, cooked and shredded
2 cans (10¾ ounces each) cream of chicken soup
2 cups sour cream
1½ cups grated sharp Cheddar cheese
1 cup chopped onion
½ cup (1 cube) butter, melted
Dash of cayenne pepper
Lemon pepper to taste
2 cups crushed corn flakes
2 tablespoons butter

Combine first eight ingredients and place in a buttered oblong pan. Top with cornflake crumbs and dot with butter. Bake at 350 degrees for 30 to 40 minutes.

BROCCOLI RICE STRATA

2 tablespoons vegetable oil
1 large onion, chopped
2 large cloves garlic, minced
½ teaspoon dried dill weed
1 teaspoon dried thyme
1 teaspoon dried oregano
½ bunch parsley, minced
2 pounds mushrooms, sliced
1 green pepper, thinly sliced
2 pounds broccoli, cut into flowerettes
½ cup unsalted cashews
½ cup freshly grated Parmesan cheese
1½ cups brown rice, cooked according to package
   directions
1 pint sour cream

In a large skillet, heat oil and sauté onion, garlic, dill, thyme, and oregano. Add parsley, mushrooms, and green pepper. Continue cooking for 2 minutes; stir in broccoli and sauté until broccoli is tender-crisp. Add nuts and cheese and remove from heat. Spread rice in the bottom of an oblong pan; layer broccoli mixture then cover with sour cream. Can be covered and refrigerated, if made ahead. Bake at 350 degrees for 20 minutes (30 minutes, if refrigerated) or until mixture is bubbling and cheese is melted.

Potato Pancakes (Latkes)

3 large potatoes, grated
1 small onion, grated
2 eggs
½ cup flour
¾ teaspoon salt
Dash pepper
Oil for frying

Combine potatoes and onion; add eggs and stir until blended. Add flour, salt, and pepper and mix well. Spoon ¼ cup mixture into ½ inch hot oil, patting lightly with a spoon to spread to desired thickness. Fry on both sides until golden brown.

Yield: 12 pancakes

Scalloped Potatoes

1 can (10¾ ounces) cream of mushroom soup
½ of a soup can of milk
3 to 4 potatoes, peeled and sliced
1 onion, chopped
1 cup grated Cheddar cheese

Combine soup and milk and pour half of mixture in bottom of square pan or casserole. Layer potatoes and onion; pour rest of soup mixture over the potatoes and top with grated cheese. Cover loosely with foil and bake at 350 degrees for 1½ hours or until potatoes are tender.

October

Nibbles and Noshes

*The highest form of bliss is
living with a certain degree of folly.*

Erasmus

Scents

There is nothing more inviting and intoxicating than to walk into a home with wonderful smells flowing out to greet you—gingerbread baking in the kitchen, simmering pots of spices and citrus peeling, potpourri, a few drops of perfume on a light bulb, fresh flowers, and scented candles.

Fun Tips

Kabobs can make snacks and finger food fun. Combine such favorites as:

* ★ Cheese cubes, ham cubes, and pickle chunks
* ★ Bite size fruit pieces and marshmallows
* ★ Zucchini slices, mushrooms, and cherry tomatoes

Halloween Dinner

Casserole in a Pumpkin Shell (p. 11)

Monster Claw Sandwiches (p. 69)

Citrus Salad (p. 160) or

Tossed Green Salad

Ghost Cake (p. 112) or

Pumpkin Dessert (p. 132)

Witches' Brew (p. 195)

Halloween

* Have a pancake dinner and play Clue or rent a spooky movie.
* Make scary sandwiches by cutting cheese into faces and melting them on an open faced cheese sandwich, a mini pizza, or an English muffin.
* Make masks using paper sacks or cut a piece of construction paper and glue a popsicle stick on it for the child to hold to his face.
* Make your own bingo game using holiday stickers. Example: B-witch, I-bat, N-pumpkin, etc. This could be done for any holiday or for bridal and baby showers.

Other

*   ★ Organize a tailgate party
*   ★ Plan a neighborhood hay ride—pick everyone up in a hay wagon, have a western potluck dinner and add western-style activities: guitar music, roping contest, and square dancing.

Nibbles and Noshes

Snacks

FRUIT-CANDIED POPCORN

1 large paper bag
Nonstick vegetable spray
10 cups unsalted popped corn
½ cup butter or margarine
¼ cup sugar
¼ cup light corn syrup
1 package (3 ounces) fruit-flavored gelatin
¼ teaspoon soda

Spray the inside of the paper bag with the nonstick spray. Place popped corn in the bag and set aside. Place butter in a 1-quart glass measuring cup and microcook on high 45 to 60 seconds, until melted. Add sugar, syrup, and gelatin; stir well. Microcook on high 3 minutes or until mixture comes to a full boil. Stir in soda (mixture will foam up). Immediately pour over popped corn. Roll down top of bag to close. Microcook on high 1½ minutes; shake bag well. Microcook on high 1 minute, shake bag vigorously. Microcook on high, 30 seconds, shake. Microcook on high, 30 seconds. Pour candied popcorn onto waxed paper to cool.

Yield: 10 cups

Play Dough

2 cups flour
1 cup salt
1 tablespoon oil
1 cup water
food coloring

Combine flour, salt, and oil, mix well. Add water and food coloring a little at a time, kneading well after each addition. Store in a plastic bag. Not edible.

Jiffy Jellies

4 envelopes unflavored gelatin (4 tablespoons gelatin)
1¼ cups cold water
1 can (6 ounces) frozen orange or grape juice concentrate, thawed

Sprinkle gelatin over water in a medium-sized saucepan. Stir over moderately low heat about 5 minutes, until gelatin is completely dissolved. Remove from heat and stir in juice. Pour into an 8-inch square baking pan and refrigerate 2 hours or more until firm. Cut into 36 squares. Covered, jellies will keep several days in the refrigerator.

Yield: 36 squares

PAINTED TOAST

Milk
Food Coloring
Bread

Put several tablespoons of milk in small paper cups. Add a few drops of food coloring and stir. With clean brush, let children create designs on the bread. Use as many different colors as desired. After painting, dry the bread in a toaster set on "light." Use to make a sandwich or spread with homemade butter.

PEANUT BUTTER CHEWS

⅓ cup peanut butter
⅓ cup honey
½ cup instant nonfat dry milk

Combine peanut butter and honey. Blend in dry milk, a small amount at a time, until thoroughly combined. Form into a roll about ¾ inch in diameter. Cut into 1-inch pieces.

Yield: 24 candies

HOMEMADE PRETZELS

1 package active dry yeast
1½ cups warm water
1 teaspoon salt
4 cups flour
1 teaspoon sugar
1 egg
Salt

Dissolve yeast in warm water. Add salt, flour, and sugar; mixing until thoroughly combined. Knead dough until smooth and elastic. Roll out on lightly floured surface into thin strips. Cut into small pieces; shape. May be formed into letters or other shapes.

Brush with beaten egg. Sprinkle with salt. Place on foil-lined cookie sheet. Bake at 425 degrees for 12 to 15 minutes.

TOASTED PUMPKIN SEEDS

½ cup butter or margarine, melted
1 teaspoon seasoned salt
3 cups pumpkin seeds, washed and dried completely

Combine butter and salt. Spread pumpkin seeds on a jelly-roll pan and drizzle with seasoned butter. Bake at 250 degrees for 1½ hours or until lightly browned.

Yield: 3 cups

PARTY DELIGHT

¼ cup green or red chili salsa
½ teaspoon cayenne pepper
2 cups vegetable oil
1 tablespoon garlic salt
1 tablespoon seasoned salt
2 tablespoons Worcestershire sauce
6 cups bite-sized corn cereal squares
10 cups bite-sized rice cereal squares
2 pounds mixed nuts
1 box (12 ounces) pretzel sticks

Mix all ingredients in a large roasting pan. Bake stirring occasionally, at 250 degrees for 1 hour and 30 minutes. Store in a glass or tin container in a cool dry place or freeze.

Yield: 6 pounds mix

CARAMEL CORN

1 package brown sugar
1 cup light corn syrup
½ cup butter
1 can (14 ounces) sweetened condensed milk
2 gallons popped corn

Bring brown sugar and corn syrup to a boil. Add butter and stir until melted; add milk. Cook, stirring constantly, to soft ball stage. Pour over popcorn and stir to coat.

MUNCHIES

    2 cups brown sugar
    2 cups butter
    4 teaspoons water
    4 tablespoons light corn syrup
    1 package (17 ounces) bite-sized rice or corn cereal
        squares
    1 cup nuts (cashews, peanuts, almonds, etc.)

Combine all ingredients except cereal and nuts and boil to soft ball stage. Pour over cereal and nuts and stir to coat. Place on waxed paper to cool.

PARTY POPCORN

    4 quarts popped corn
    2 cups whole nuts (pecans, cashews, peanuts, etc.)
    3 cups miniature marshmallows
    1½ cups fruit gum drops
    1 cup butter or margarine
    1⅓ cups sugar
    ½ cup light corn syrup
    1 teaspoon vanilla

Mix popcorn, nuts, marshmallows, and gum drops in large mixing bowl. Melt butter in heavy saucepan and add sugar and corn syrup. Bring to a boil, stirring and simmer 3 minutes. Add vanilla, blend well. Pour over the popcorn mixture, mix well. Let stand 2 minutes to cool. With hands dampened in cool water, mold into desired shape. Arrange on baking sheet to set. Wrap in plastic wrap and store in cool place.

INDIAN CANDY CORN

1 box (10.9 ounces) popped corn cereal
1 cup mixed nuts
½ cup butter or margarine
1 cup granulated sugar
½ cup light corn syrup
1 teaspoon vanilla extract
1 teaspoon baking soda
1 cup candy corn

Preheat oven to 250 degrees. Combine cereal and nuts in a greased, large, shallow baking pan. In a saucepan bring butter, sugar, and corn syrup to a boil and cook for 5 minutes. Remove from heat; add vanilla and soda. Pour caramel mixture over cereal and nuts; stir well. Bake for 1 hour, stirring every 15 minutes. Pour onto waxed paper and break apart. Allow to cool and add candy corn. Store in airtight container.

Yield: 10 cups

PUPPY CHOW

1 package (12 ounces) chocolate chips
1 cup peanut butter
½ cup butter or margarine
1 package (12 ounces) bite-sized rice cereal squares
Powdered sugar (about 2 cups)

Combine chips, peanut butter, and butter; melt. Cool a few minutes and pour over cereal. Put powdered sugar in paper bag and add cereal mixture. Shake and coat cereal.

SAVORY PRETZELS

¾ cup oil
1 package (one ounce) ranch dressing mix
½ teaspoon dill weed
½ teaspoon lemon pepper
1 pound Bavarian Pretzels (Bulk Foods) broken

Mix oil and dry seasonings; add pretzels and stir to coat. Marinate pretzels 15 to 30 minutes. Drain on a paper towel. Bake at 300 degrees for 15 minutes.

Yield: 1 pound

SUMMER SAUSAGE

2 pounds ground beef (regular)
1 cup cold water
2 teaspoons liquid smoke
½ teaspoon pepper
¼ teaspoon garlic powder
½ teaspoon onion powder
1 teaspoon mustard seed
2 tablespoons plus 2 teaspoons Morton's Tender Quick

Mix all ingredients together, making sure the seasonings are well distributed. Divide mixture and roll into two meat logs. Place meat on shiny side of aluminum foil sheets and wrap each log securely and individually. Let stand for 24 hours in the refrigerator. Before baking, pierce holes in the foil on the bottom and sides with a sharp fork. This allows grease to drain out during baking. Place on a broiler pan and bake at 350 degrees for 1 hour and 15 minutes. Serve hot or cold. Keep refrigerated.

Yield: 2 logs

STRAWBERRY CREAM POPS

1 cup sugar
½ cup water
4 cups strawberries
⅓ cup orange juice
2 tablespoons lemon juice
1 cup heavy cream, whipped

In saucepan, combine sugar and water. Boil 5 minutes; cool. Puree strawberries, orange juice, and lemon juice in blender. Add sugar water and fold in whipped cream. Pour into small paper cups. Freeze until partially set (1 hour). Place sticks in center of cup and freeze well.

Yield: 14 pops

PINK POPCORN

2 quarts popped popcorn
¾ cup sugar
¼ cup light corn syrup
3 tablespoons water
1 tablespoon red cinnamon candy

Place popped corn in large buttered bowl. Combine remaining ingredients in small saucepan. Heat slowly, stirring constantly, to boiling point. Cook without stirring to 272 degrees—soft crack stage. Remove from heat and drizzle over popcorn, stirring to coat. When well mixed, pour onto buttered cookie sheet and bake at 325 degrees for about 10 minutes. Separate kernels when cool.

Yield: 2 quarts

Orange Cartwheel

1 orange
1 tablespoon powdered sugar
Flaked coconut (tinted, if desired), toasted coconut,
    or granola

Peel orange and cut into round slices. Place on a plate and sprinkle with powdered sugar. Let stand several minutes. Sprinkle coconut or granola over oranges and enjoy.

Yield: 1 serving

Banana Pops

3 tablespoons unsweetened cocoa
2 tablespoons honey
½ teaspoon vanilla
1 tablespoon milk
3 firm bananas
½ cup granola, coconut, wheat germ, or crushed nuts
6 popsicle sticks

Mix cocoa, honey, vanilla, and milk. Peel bananas and cut in half, crosswise. Place popsicle stick in the cut end of each banana. Roll the bananas in the cocoa mixture and then in the topping. Place on a waxed paper-lined plate and freeze for at least 2 hours.

Yield: 6 servings

November

The Main Event

May the warm winds of heaven
Blow softly on this house
May the Great Spirit
Bless all who enter here.

Indian Saying

May your moccasins make
Happy tracks in many snows
And the rainbow always
touch your shoulder.

Indian Saying

Nuts

This is the time of year for nuts. Nuts can enhance many simple foods and make them sublime. Try a few of these ideas:

* ★ Toasted pecans sprinkled on fresh fruit salad or spinach salad.
* ★ Pine nuts in green salads or as a garnish for soups.

* Macadamia nuts or toasted almonds in chicken salads and sandwiches.
* Toasted hazelnuts lavished over ice cream sundaes or in apple salads.
* Chopped pecans as a coating for fish and chicken.

Fun Tips

* A good rule of thumb for cooking fish: Measure the fish at its thickest part with a ruler. Cook the fish, by any method, for 10 minutes per inch. Fish continues to cook for a minute or two after it is out of the oven.
* Tie a lemon half in a cheesecloth bag to serve with fish. The bag catches all the seeds!

An Indian Pow Wow

Navajo Tacos (p. 22)

Colossal Chip Cookies (p. 266)

Indian Candy Corn (p. 231)

Indian Summer Sipper (p. 195)

Thanksgiving

* ★ Trace your hand and write on each finger something you are thankful for.
* ★ Give each person 5 pieces of candy corn (represents all the pilgrims had in storage to eat one winter) and tell a Thanksgiving story.
* ★ Make Pioneer Honey Candy and relate a pioneer story.
* ★ Make an "I Am Thankful" box and bury or hide it until next year.
* ★ Design turkeys using pine cones fitted with construction paper and fuzzy pipe-cleaners. Can be used as place card holders.
* ★ Create napkin rings by cutting toilet paper rolls into thirds and wrapping them with crepe paper.
* ★ Plan a "leftover" dinner party and serve turkey soup, salad, and hot bread.

The Main Event

Meats

SAUCY CHICKEN

6 chicken breasts or other pieces
Salt, pepper, and garlic salt
¼ teaspoon celery seed
¼ cup vinegar
¼ cup Worcestershire sauce
1 cup catsup
1 teaspoon Tabasco sauce
1 onion, finely chopped
¼ cup brown sugar
1 cup boiling water

Place chicken in an oblong pan and sprinkle with salt, pepper, and garlic salt. Brown at 400 degrees for ½ hour. Combine rest of ingredients and pour over chicken and bake at 350 degrees for 1½ hours.

Yield: 6 servings

CHICKEN SQUARES

1 cup diced, cooked chicken
1 package (3 ounces) cream cheese, softened
1 can (4 ounces) mushrooms
1 tube (8-serving size) crescent rolls
1 can (10¾ ounces) cream of chicken soup

Mix chicken, cream cheese, and mushrooms together. Roll out each crescent roll and place a tablespoon of chicken mixture in the center. Fold each triangle to the center, slightly overlapping, and seal edges. Bake at 350 degrees for 10 minutes. Warm soup and serve as a sauce.

Yield: 8 servings

Note: Turkey could be substituted for the chicken.

CREAM SAUCE FOR ANY CHICKEN

2 cups milk
2 packages (8 ounces each) cream cheese, softened
½ cup Parmesan cheese
½ teaspoon salt
½ teaspoon garlic powder

Heat milk, add rest of ingredients and warm thoroughly. Do not allow sauce to come to a boil. Serve over chicken.

CHICKEN WELLINGTON

1 package (17 ounces) frozen puff pastry dough
8 boneless chicken breasts
2 tablespoons butter
2 tablespoons finely minced green onions (white part only)
1 pound mushrooms, finely chopped
1 tablespoon chopped parsley
Salt and pepper
1 egg
½ teaspoon salt

Remove puff pastry dough from freezer, let thaw about 20 minutes; for the tenderest pastry keep the dough cold to the touch. In a medium saucepan melt 2 tablespoons butter; add green onions. Stir over medium heat until soft but not browned. Add mushrooms. Cook over high heat stirring often, until dry. Remove from heat and add parsley. Season with salt and pepper. Refrigerate to cool completely.

Trim and remove the skin from the chicken breasts. Using a meat mallet or a rolling pin, flatten each until about ¼ inch thick. Set aside. Lightly grease a baking sheet. Roll out pastry to a rectangle, each sheet should be about 18 inches by 12 inches. Cut each sheet into 4 squares. Place a well rounded tablespoon of the mushroom mixture on each chicken breast. Roll up chicken with mushroom mixture inside, tucking in ends and sealing well. Place each on a square of pastry. Combine the egg and the ½ teaspoon salt; brush the edges of the dough with the egg mixture. Fold up to the center and press lightly to seal. Brush with egg glaze. Cut leaves and other decorative shapes from leftover dough and attach to top of pastry with egg glaze. Use a sharp knife to cut vent in top of dough to let steam escape.

Chicken Wellington can be prepared to this point 8 hours ahead, covered and refrigerated. Preheat oven to 425 degrees ½ hour before serving. Bake Chicken Wellington 25 minutes at 425 degrees until pastry is lightly browned. Serve immediately with a chicken mushroom gravy.

Yield: 8 servings

CASHEW CHICKEN

1 pound boneless chicken breasts, cut in thin strips
2 tablespoons soy sauce
1 tablespoon cornstarch
2 tablespoons oil
1 small onion, peeled, chopped
½ pound mushrooms, trimmed, sliced thin lengthwise
    through stems
2 tablespoons oil
1 small cabbage, shredded (about 4 cups)
1 teaspoon sugar
1 package (6 ounces) cashew nuts
1 teaspoon cornstarch
¼ cup soy sauce
1 can (3 ounces) Chinese fried noodles

In a small bowl, place chicken strips with soy sauce and cornstarch. Blend well. Let stand at room temperature for 15 minutes. Heat oil in wok over high heat. Add chicken strips and stir-fry until white and firm. Add onion and mushrooms. Continue to stir-fry vegetables until they are soft. Place in a separate bowl. Add remaining oil to wok. Stir in cabbage and sugar. Stir-fry about 3 to 4 minutes until cabbage is crisp-tender. Return chicken and vegetable mixture to wok. Add cashews, toss to combine with cabbage. Dissolve cornstarch in soy sauce. Stir into chicken-cashew mixture. Cover and steam for 1 minute. Uncover and stir until sauce is thickened. Sprinkle with Chinese fried noodles just before serving.

Yield: 6 to 8 servings

Busy Day Chicken Breasts

6 to 8 skinless chicken breasts, deboned
6 to 8 slices bacon, partially cooked
1 package chipped beef
1 pint sour cream
1 can (10¾ ounces) cream of mushroom soup

Grease the bottom of an oblong baking pan. Wrap each chicken breast with a slice of bacon. Layer chipped beef on the bottom of the pan and then the chicken breasts. Mix sour cream and soup and pour over chicken. Cover pan and refrigerate 12 to 24 hours. Bake at 250 degrees for 3 hours.

Yield: 6 to 8 servings

Marinated Turkey Steaks

1 cup oil
1 cup soy sauce
2 cups lemon–lime carbonated beverage
5 to 6 pounds turkey steaks

Combine oil, soy sauce, and lemon–lime carbonated beverage. Pour over turkey steaks in an oblong glass pan. Marinate turkey for 8 hours in the refrigerator. Charcoal grill steaks.

Yield: 6 to 8 servings

Note: Also great with chicken.

BURGER SUPREME

1½ pounds ground beef
3 tablespoons water
1 teaspoon salt
½ teaspoon ground sage
¼ cup chopped green onion
1 tablespoon prepared horseradish
1 tablespoon prepared mustard
1 package (3 ounces) cream cheese, softened

Mix ground beef, water, salt, and sage together. Divide mixture into halves. Shape each half into a large patty (about 8 inches in diameter) on waxed paper. Mix remaining ingredients. Spread mixture over one patty, within ½ inch of edge. Top with remaining patty, removing waxed paper. Seal edges firmly.

Grill patty about 4 inches from medium coals, turning 2 or 3 times, 12 to 14 minutes on each side. Cut into wedges. Garnish with green onions and cherry tomatoes.

Yield: 6 servings

MEAT LOAF

½ cup chopped onion, browned
1½ pounds ground beef
½ pound lean ground pork
1 cup bread crumbs
1 to 2 teaspoons salt
¼ teaspoon pepper
¼ teaspoon allspice
2 eggs
⅔ cup milk

Combine all ingredients and bake in a greased 8-inch ring mold at 350 degrees for 1 hour. Unmold and fill center with creamed peas. Serve with Snow-Time Surprise Salad (p. 182).

Yield: 6 servings

INDIVIDUAL MEAT LOAVES

¾ pound ground beef
⅛ teaspoon pepper
½ cup evaporated milk
1 tablespoon chopped onion
¾ teaspoon salt
½ cup dry bread crumbs

Lightly mix all ingredients together. Avoid over-mixing. Shape into 4 small individual loaves and place side-by-side in a casserole dish. Pour barbecue sauce over loaves and bake at 350 degrees for 40 minutes. Serve with individual pots of baked beans.

Barbecue Sauce:

¼ cup catsup
3 tablespoons vinegar
1 teaspoon brown sugar
1 tablespoon beef base

MEATBALLS

1 pound lean ground beef
½ pound lean ground pork or sausage
½ cup chopped onion
1 tablespoon Worcestershire sauce
1 teaspoon salt
1½ cups applesauce
1 cup dry bread crumbs

Combine all ingredients and mix well. Divide mixture and roll into balls. Place in greased muffin pans. Bake at 350 degrees for 30 to 40 minutes or until done.

Yield: 16 meatballs

STEAK PITAS

2 tablespoons oil
1 pound sirloin steak, thinly sliced
1 green pepper, thinly sliced
1 onion, chopped
1 pound mushrooms, sliced
1 tablespoon steak sauce
2 tomatoes, chopped
Dash of salt and pepper
1 cup Mozzarella cheese, grated
Lettuce
6 pita bread pockets

Measure oil into wok; heat on high temperature. Add steak, cook until done. Add green pepper and onion and stir-fry for about 1 minute. Add mushrooms and steak sauce, stir-fry for about 2 minutes. Add Mozzarella cheese and melt. Cut pita bread in half. Stuff with lettuce, tomato, and meat mixture. Serve immediately.

Yield: 6 servings

SAURBRATEN

1 (4 pound) boneless beef round rump roast
2 tablespoons cooking oil
½ cup chopped onion
½ cup chopped carrot
¼ cup chopped celery
Marinade (recipe below)

Prepare marinade. Place meat in a plastic bag or airtight container. Pour marinade over meat, close container. Refrigerate 72 hours, turning meat occasionally. Remove meat; pat excess moisture from meat. Strain marinade, set aside. In Dutch Oven, brown meat on all sides in hot oil. Drain off fat. Add marinade, onion, carrot, and celery. Cover, simmer at least 2 hours or until meat is tender. Transfer meat to platter, keep warm. Reserve cooking liquid and vegetables. Make gravy with cooking liquid.

Yield: 12 servings

Marinade:

Combine 3 cups water; ¾ cups red wine vinegar; 2 medium onions, sliced; 1 lemon, sliced; 12 whole cloves; 6 black peppercorns, crushed; 4 bay leaves, crushed; 2 tablespoons sugar; 1 tablespoon salt; and ¼ teaspoon ground ginger.

SWISS BLISS

2 tablespoons butter
2 pounds round steak or chuck steak, cut into serving-sized pieces
1 envelope dry onion soup mix
½ pound mushrooms, sliced
½ green pepper, sliced
1 can (1 pound) tomatoes, drained and chopped (reserve juice)
Salt and pepper
½ cup juice from tomatoes
1 tablespoon steak sauce
1 tablespoon cornstarch

Spread center of large piece of aluminum foil with butter. Arrange meat on foil, slightly overlapping each portion. Sprinkle with onion soup mix, mushrooms, green pepper, tomatoes, salt, and pepper. Mix steak sauce and cornstarch and pour over meat and vegetables. Wrap foil around meat double folding edges. Seal tightly. Bake at 350 degrees for 2 hours. Can be done on a barbecue.

Yield: 4 to 6 servings

TERIYAKI STEAK

1 cup soy sauce
1 cup water
¼ pound fresh ginger root, peeled and grated
3 cloves garlic, minced
6 pounds steak (for barbecue)

Combine soy sauce, water, ginger, and garlic in a large glass pan; add steak. Marinate steak for 8 hours in the refrigerator. Charcoal grill steaks.

Yield: 8 to 10 servings

ANNA'S STEAK

1 round steak, cubed
Flour to coat
2 tablespoons butter
1 onion, chopped
1 can (10¾ ounces) cream of mushroom soup

Place flour and steak in a paper sack and shake well to coat meat. Brown in butter. Place meat in a casserole dish and cover with onion and mushroom soup. Cover casserole dish and bake ½ hour at 300 degrees; turn oven to 250 degrees and continue cooking for 1½ hours.

TRIMMED BRISKET

Brisket (allow one pound meat for every 5 people)
1 envelope dry onion soup mix
¼ cup soy sauce
⅛ cup Worcestershire sauce
1½ cups hickory barbecue sauce.

Place meat on large piece of aluminum foil; sprinkle with soup mix; pour soy sauce and Worcestershire sauce over meat. Wrap foil around meat and seal tightly. Place in a roasting pan. Bake for 8 hours at 275 degrees. One-half hour before serving slice meat and cover with barbecue sauce; cover and cook for ½ hour.

BEEF STROGANOFF

1½ pounds top round steak, sliced ¼ inch thick
4 tablespoons flour
1 teaspoon salt
¼ teaspoon pepper
¼ cup butter
1½ cups chopped onion
½ clove garlic, minced
¼ cup water
1 can (10½ ounces) beef consommé
1 pound fresh mushrooms, washed
1 cup sour cream

Trim fat from meat and cut into strips about 1 inch wide and 2 inches long. Combine flour, salt, and pepper in a paper lunch sack; add meat strips and shake until well coated. Melt butter and cook onion and garlic until lightly browned; place in a separate bowl. Place meat strips in a pan and brown on all sides. Add the water, consommé, and onion. Cover and simmer for 30 minutes. Add mushrooms and continue cooking until meat is tender. Just before serving, stir in sour cream. Serve over buttered noodles.

Yield: 6 servings

BARBECUE RIBS

2 jars (4½ ounces each) strained peaches or apricots
    (baby food)
⅓ cup catsup
⅓ cup vinegar
2 tablespoons soy sauce
½ cup brown sugar
2 teaspoons ginger
2 cloves garlic, minced
Dash pepper
4 pounds spareribs

Mix fruit, catsup, vinegar, soy sauce, brown sugar, ginger, and garlic; set aside. Rub ribs on both sides with salt and pepper. Place ribs, meat side up, in a foil-lined shallow pan. Bake at 450 degrees for 15 minutes; spoon off fat. Pour sauce over ribs. Continue baking at 350 degrees for 1½ hours, basting with sauce frequently. Cut in serving pieces. Finger-Licking Good.

Yield: 4 servings

HAM ROLLS

1 package frozen spinach, thawed and drained well
1 pint cottage cheese, drained
¼ cup green onions, sliced
½ teaspoon dry mustard
2 eggs, slightly beaten
1 tablespoon flour
Salt and pepper to taste
½ pint sour cream
12 slices ham, thinly sliced

Mix first eight ingredients together and place a large spoonful of mixture on each slice of ham; roll each and secure with a toothpick. Place in a baking pan. Pour sauce over ham rolls and bake at 300 degrees for 40 minutes.

Note: Cooked rice may be used to extend filling.

Sauce:
1 can (10¾ ounces) cream of mushroom soup
½ pint sour cream

Mix well.

COMPANY HAM

1 (5 to 8 pound) precooked boneless ham
1 teaspoon whole cloves
1 cup apple cider
1 teaspoon ground cinnamon
½ teaspoon nutmeg
Pineapple slices
Maraschino cherries

Stud ham with cloves. Place ham in a browning bag and put into heavy pan. Pour cider over ham and sprinkle with spices. Secure browning bag. Bake at 325 degrees for 15 to 20 minutes per pound of ham. Remove and discard juices. Garnish ham with pineapple slices and cherries secured by toothpicks. Serve immediately.

Yield: 12 to 15 servings

Microwave Oven: Prepare ham following above directions. Microcook for 1 to 1½ hours on medium power (50%) level.

FRENCH-FRIED LIVER

Liver, frozen for easy slicing
French dressing
Beaten egg
Cracker crumbs

Cut liver in ½ inch strips. Let stand, covered, in French dressing for ½ hour; drain. Dip in beaten egg and roll in cracker crumbs. Fry in hot fat, 360 degrees, until browned. Drain on paper towels; serve hot.

Ham Loaf

4 cups ground cooked ham
½ cup pork sausage
1 cup bread crumbs
2 eggs, beaten
½ teaspoon allspice
1 tablespoon mustard
¼ cup chopped parsley
¼ cup chopped green pepper
2 tablespoons minced onion
1 can (10¾ ounces) tomato soup

Mix all ingredients together and bake in a greased ring mold at 350 degrees for one hour. Let stand 5 to 10 minutes before removing from pan. Serve with Horseradish sauce.

Yield: 8 to 10 servings

Horseradish Sauce:

½ cup cottage cheese
½ cup whipping cream, whipped
1 to 2 tablespoons prepared horseradish

Whip cottage cheese until smooth and fold into cream. Fold in horseradish. Chill.

MARYLAND CRAB CAKES

    1 pound lump crab meat
    2 slices white bread, crusts removed
    1 egg
    1 tablespoon mayonnaise
    1 teaspoon Dijon mustard
    Salt and black pepper
    1 teaspoon Old Bay Seasoning, optional
    3 tablespoons butter, if frying
    Tartar sauce

Pick over the crab thoroughly, removing any bits of shell. Break the bread into ¼-inch pieces. In a bowl, beat the egg with the mayonnaise. Add the seasonings and bread pieces. Add crab and mix gently with your hands. Form into four thick, round patties and refrigerate for at least 2 hours. If broiling, preheat the broiler and then broil the cakes on a buttered rack for 5 minutes on each side. If you choose to pan-fry them, melt the butter in a skillet and pan-fry them over medium heat for 3 to 4 minutes per side. Serve with Tartar Sauce (recipe follows).

Yield: 4 servings

TARTAR SAUCE

    1 cup mayonnaise
    2 teaspoons Dijon mustard
    2 teaspoons chopped capers
    2 teaspoons chopped dill pickles
    2 teaspoons chopped fresh chives
    2 teaspoons chopped fresh tarragon
    Black pepper to taste

Combine mayonnaise, mustard, capers, dill pickles, chives, tarragon. Season with black pepper to taste.

VEAL BIRDS

2 pounds ½ inch veal steak
1¼ teaspoons salt
Dash pepper
3 cups dry bread cubes
3 tablespoons melted butter or margarine
2½ tablespoons chopped onion
¾ teaspoon salt
½ teaspoon poultry seasoning
Dash pepper
2 teaspoons water

Pound steak thoroughly with meat mallet to ¼ inch thick; sprinkle with salt and pepper. Cut in 3x5-inch pieces. To make stuffing, combine the remaining ingredients; add water to moisten (about 2 teaspoons). Top veal with stuffing. Roll; fasten with toothpicks. Brown in hot fat; add ⅓ cup hot water; cover tightly and cook slowly till tender, about 1 hour, turning occasionally.

Yield: 6 servings

December

Nutcracker Sweets

Remember, Happiness is as a butterfly
Which when pursued is always beyond our
Reach, but which, if you will sit
Down quietly may alight upon you.

Hawthorne

Christmas Decorating

Decorating at Christmas time is the event most anticipated all year long. Wreaths are an important part of our
Christmas treasures. Wreath making is an ancient art that orig-
inated about a thousand years before Christ. The scholar wore
a crown of ivy; the statesman, laurel; and the warrior, oak
leaves. Only noble men wore these crowns. At Christmas the
wreath is symbolic of immortality.

To add to the festive fragrance of Christmas, tuck herb
bundles into the Christmas tree; use juniper berries, pine
cones, and rose hips everywhere; drape the mantel, staircases,
and doorways with fresh pine boughs, holly, and mistletoe; toss
herbs, cinnamon, or hickory chips on the fire.

Fun Tips

★ Did you know . . .
There is a town named:
Snowflake, Arizona
Joy, Illinois
Evergreen, Alabama
Santa Claus, Indiana
Noel, Missouri
Silverbell, Arizona
North Pole, Colorado
North Pole, New York

Holiday Brunch

Sunrise Frappe Fruit Cup (p. 202) or

Grenadine Grapefruit (p. 144)

Brunch Omelet (p. 5) or

German Pancakes with lemon (p. 96)

Dutch Apple Muffins (p. 90)

Ice Cream balls rolled in pecans and
served on a bed of chocolate or raspberry sauce

Cider-Citrus Punch (p. 203) or

Mint Hot Chocolate Malt Mix (p. 197)

Yulenog (p. 199)

Christmas

* Collect pine boughs and pine cones for wreaths, swags, and sprays.

* Hold an open house on Christmas Eve or a few days before for "Tired Santas."

* Choose someone who is alone and surprise them with the Twelve Days of Christmas.

* Have a cookie party—make gingerbread men ahead of time and let children ice and decorate them with raisins, sprinkles etc. Give a prize for the best gingerbread man.

* Hang up the stockings and read last year's resolutions.

* Make a Yule log as a family. Decorate a small log using pine boughs, berries, pine cones, and ribbon.

* Create your own wrapping paper by using sponge or vegetable print on white or brown butcher paper.

* Leave hay or carrots for Santa's reindeer.

* Hide an almond in the cake for Christmas Eve to determine who opens the first gift the next morning.

Nutcracker Sweets

Cookies

APPLESAUCE COOKIES

¾ cup shortening
1½ cups sugar
3 eggs
1 can (16 ounces) applesauce
3 cups flour
1½ teaspoons soda
¾ teaspoon cinnamon
¾ teaspoon salt
¾ teaspoon nutmeg
¾ teaspoon cloves
1½ cups oatmeal
1 cup raisins
1 cup chocolate chips

Cream shortening and sugar; add eggs and mix well. Add sifted dry ingredients alternately with applesauce. Mix in oatmeal, raisins, and chocolate chips. Drop onto a cookie sheet lined with cooking parchment, and bake at 400 degrees for 9 to 12 minutes.

SOFT GINGERSNAPS

¾ cup shortening
1 cup brown sugar
¼ cup molasses
1 large egg
2¼ cups flour
2 teaspoons soda
½ teaspoon salt
1 teaspoon ginger
1 teaspoon cinnamon
½ teaspoon cloves
Sugar

Cream shortening, sugar, and molasses; add egg. Stir in sifted dry ingredients. Chill. Shape dough into balls and roll in sugar. Bake at 375 degrees for 10 to 12 minutes.

Note: Store with a slice of bread to keep cookies soft.

MELT-AWAY COOKIES

1 cup butter (no substitutions)
¾ cup cornstarch
⅓ cup confectioners' sugar
1 cup flour
Frosting (recipe below)

Cream butter; gradually add cornstarch and sugar. Blend in flour, mixing thoroughly. Drop mixture by spoonfuls onto ungreased baking sheet. Bake at 325 degrees for 10 to 12 minutes until done and lightly browned. Cool and frost.

Frosting:

1 package (3 ounces) cream cheese, softened
1 teaspoon vanilla
1 cup confectioners' sugar

Beat until thoroughly blended.

Pumpkin Waffle Iron Cookies

1⅓ cups sugar
½ cup shortening
2 eggs, beaten
1 cup pumpkin
1 teaspoon vanilla
1 teaspoon salt
2 teaspoons baking powder
¾ teaspoon cinnamon
¾ teaspoon nutmeg
¼ teaspoon ginger
2½ cups flour
½ cup chopped nuts

Cream sugar and shortening till fluffy. Add eggs and blend well; add vanilla and pumpkin. Combine dry ingredients; add to creamed mixture. Add nuts. Place small balls of dough on hot waffle iron about 3 inches apart. Bake and frost, if desired.

Cherry Macaroon Cookies

1½ cups sugar
1⅓ cups shortening
1 teaspoon salt
1½ teaspoons almond extract
2 eggs
3½ cups flour
2 teaspoons baking powder
2 teaspoons soda
1 cup chopped maraschino cherries
1½ cups coconut

Cream sugar and shortening, add salt, extract, and eggs. Add sifted dry ingredients and mix well. Add cherries and coconut. Drop by spoonfuls onto lightly greased cookie sheet. Bake at 375 degrees for 15 minutes.

SOFT SUGAR COOKIES

1 cup butter or margarine
1 cup sugar
2 eggs, beaten
2 teaspoons vanilla
3 cups flour
½ teaspoon soda
½ teaspoon salt
1 teaspoon baking powder
½ cup canned milk

Cream butter and sugar. Add eggs and vanilla and mix well. Add sifted dry ingredients alternately with milk. Chill a few hours or overnight. Roll and cut into cookies. Bake at 375 degrees for 7 minutes until lightly browned on bottom only (the top shouldn't be browned). If the dough is sticky, add flour as you roll it out. Frost and decorate.

Variation: Lemon extract could be used instead of vanilla.

TOFFEE COOKIES

1 cup shortening
1 cup brown sugar
1 egg
1 teaspoon vanilla
2 cups flour
1 package (6 ounces) chocolate chips
½ cup finely chopped nuts

Cream shortening and sugar; add egg and vanilla, mixing well. Stir in flour. Spread batter into a 10x13-inch rectangle on a greased cookie sheet. Bake at 350 degrees for 15 minutes. Remove from oven and sprinkle chocolate chips over the top. When chips are softened, spread evenly over entire surface. Sprinkle with nuts and cut into bars.

SOFT OATMEAL COOKIES

2 cups sugar
2 cups raisins
1½ cups water
1 cup oil
1 teaspoon soda
3 cups flour
3 cups quick oatmeal
1 cup nuts
1 tablespoon cinnamon
1 tablespoon nutmeg
1 teaspoon baking powder
1 teaspoon ground cloves
1 teaspoon salt

Mix sugar, raisins, water, oil, and soda in a saucepan and bring to a boil. Boil 4 minutes. Meanwhile mix dry ingredients and nuts together. Pour liquid into flour mixture. Mix well.

Drop by spoonfuls onto cookie sheet. Bake at 375 degrees for 10 minutes. Store in an air-tight container.

COLOSSAL CHIP COOKIES

¾ cup shortening
1 cup brown sugar
½ cup sugar
1 egg
¼ cup water
1 teaspoon almond or vanilla extract
1 teaspoon salt
½ teaspoon soda
1 cup flour
1 cup chopped walnuts
3 cups quick oatmeal
1 package (7 ounces) chocolate kisses candy

Cream shortening and sugars together; add egg, water, extract, salt, soda, and flour. Mix well. Stir in nuts and oats. Fold in chocolate kisses. Place ⅓ cup batter for each cookie on baking sheets. Bake at 350 degrees for 12 minutes.

Yield: 14 cookies

MINT SURPRISE COOKIES

½ cup butter
½ cup shortening
1 cup sugar
½ cup brown sugar
2 eggs
2 tablespoons water
1 teaspoon vanilla
3 cups flour
1 teaspoon soda
½ teaspoon salt
1 package (9 ounces) chocolate mint wafers

Cream butter, shortening, and sugars; add eggs, water, and vanilla, mixing well. Stir in sifted dry ingredients. Chill at least 2 hours. Shape cookies by enclosing each wafer in about 1 tablespoon dough. Place on greased cookie sheet about 2 inches apart. Bake at 375 degrees for 10 to 12 minutes.

AUNT LEONA'S BROWNIES

2 squares (1 ounce each) unsweetened chocolate, melted
½ cup butter, melted
1 cup sugar
3 eggs
½ cup flour
2 teaspoons vanilla
Pinch salt
1 cup nuts

Combine chocolate, butter, and sugar. Add one egg at a time, beating well after each. Add flour, vanilla, salt, and nuts. Pour into well greased square pan. Bake at 325 degrees for 40 minutes.

Cover with chocolate frosting and finely chopped nuts.

PRUNE SPICE SNAPS

1 cup shortening
1 cup sugar
1 cup molasses
3 eggs
2 cups prunes, cut into fourths
1½ cups walnuts
4½ cups flour
1 teaspoon baking soda
1 teaspoon salt
½ teaspoon nutmeg
1 teaspoon cinnamon
¼ teaspoon cloves

Frosting:
¾ cup powdered sugar
¾ teaspoon water

Cream shortening, sugar, and molasses; add eggs, prunes, and walnuts, mixing well. Add sifted dry ingredients. Chill. Divide dough into 4 pieces. Roll each portion into a rectangle 14x4 inches. Bake 2 rectangles at a time at 400 degrees for 12 to 15 minutes. Mix sugar and water. Frost while bars are warm. Cut diagonally into 1½ inch bars.

Yield: 4 dozen bars

FRESH-FRUIT COOKIE TARTS

1 roll refrigerated oatmeal-raisin, peanut butter, or sugar
    cookie dough
Desired fruit, such as strawberries, bananas, seedless
    grapes, oranges, kiwi, or apples
1 can (16 ounces) vanilla or tapioca pudding
Raisins or toasted coconut, optional

Preheat oven to 375 degrees. Unwrap roll of cookie
dough. With a sharp knife, cut roll into 9 equal slices. Place
4 inches apart on ungreased cookie sheets. Flatten slightly.
Bake at 375 degrees for 9 to 11 minutes or until cookies are
light golden brown. Cool on rack. Just before serving, cut
desired fruits. Spoon some vanilla or tapioca pudding over
each cookie, spreading it to the edges. Decorate cookies with
cut-up fruit. If desired, add raisins or toasted coconut. Serve
immediately.

Yield: 9 cookies

CUT-OUT GINGERBREAD COOKIES

⅓ cup shortening
1 cup brown sugar
1½ cups molasses
½ cup cold water
7 cups flour
1 teaspoon salt
1 teaspoon allspice
1 teaspoon ginger
1 teaspoon cloves
1 teaspoon cinnamon
2 teaspoons soda dissolved in 3 tablespoons cold water

Cream shortening and sugar; add molasses and water, mixing well. Add sifted dry ingredients alternately with soda water. Chill dough. Roll out to ½ inch thick and cut with cookie cutters. Place on lightly greased baking sheet. Bake at 350 degrees for 15 to 18 minutes.

Yield: 2½ dozen

Note: Store with a slice of bread to keep cookies soft.

CARROT COOKIES

½ cup butter
1 cup sugar
1 egg
1 teaspoon vanilla
1 teaspoon lemon extract
1 cup shredded carrots, cooked, cooled
2 cups flour
2 teaspoons baking powder
½ teaspoon salt
½ cup oatmeal
1 cup chopped walnuts

Cream butter and sugar; add egg, vanilla, and lemon extract. Beat well. Stir in carrots. Add sifted dry ingredients, oatmeal, and nuts; mix well. Drop onto greased cookie sheet and bake at 350 degrees for 8 to 10 minutes. Glaze, if desired.

THUMBPRINT COOKIES

¼ cup shortening
¼ cup butter
¼ cup brown sugar
1 egg yolk, reserve white
½ teaspoon vanilla
1 cup flour
¼ teaspoon salt
Finely chopped nuts
Jelly, candied fruit, or icing

Cream shortening, butter, and sugar; add egg yolk and vanilla. Blend well. Add flour and salt and mix thoroughly. Roll dough into small balls and dip in slightly beaten egg white; roll in nuts. Place on ungreased cookie sheet. Bake at 375 degrees for 5 minutes. Remove from oven and quickly press centers with thumb; return to oven and bake 8 minutes longer. Fill with jelly, candied fruit, or icing.

CHOCOLATE CHIP COOKIES

1 cup butter-flavored shortening
¾ cup brown sugar
¾ cup sugar
2 eggs
1 teaspoon vanilla
1 teaspoon soda
1 teaspoon salt
2¼ cups flour
1 package (12 ounces) chocolate chips
½ cup chopped nuts

Cream shortening and sugars; add eggs and vanilla and beat well. Sift together soda, salt, and flour and add to sugar mixture. Add chocolate chips and nuts. Drop by spoonfuls onto ungreased cookie sheets. Bake at 375 degrees for 10 minutes.

Note: For freshness, store cookies with a slice of bread.

PECAN BALLS

½ cup butter or margarine
½ cup plus 2 tablespoons shortening
1 cup powdered sugar
2 teaspoons vanilla
2½ cups cake flour
1 cup pecans

Cream butter, shortening, and sugar; add vanilla. Stir in flour; add pecans. Roll dough into balls and place on an ungreased cookie sheet. Bake at 325 degrees for about 15 minutes (don't let cookies brown).

TURTLE BARS

1 package (14 ounces) caramels
⅓ cup evaporated milk
1 package German chocolate cake mix
¾ cup melted butter
⅓ cup evaporated milk
1 cup chopped pecans
1 cup semisweet chocolate pieces

In glass bowl, combine caramels and ⅓ cup evaporated milk. Microcook on high for 3 minutes. Stir until smooth and fully melted. Set aside.

Combine cake mix, butter, ⅓ cup evaporated milk and nuts. Mix until dough is smooth. Press half of dough into a greased and floured baking dish. Bake at 350 degrees for 6 to 10 minutes. Sprinkle chocolate pieces over baked crust. Spread caramel mixture over chocolate pieces. Place remaining dough over the caramel mixture. Bake at 350 degrees for 15 to 18 minutes. Cool, then refrigerate to set caramel layer. Cut into bars.

Yield: 36 bars

No-Bake Chocolate Marshmallow Roll Cookies

1 egg
1 cup powdered sugar
3 tablespoons butter, melted
3 squares semisweet chocolate, melted
1 teaspoon vanilla
8 graham crackers, crushed
36 colored marshmallows
  OR 1 package miniature marshmallows
1 cup walnuts
Extra graham crackers crushed for rolling

Beat egg well, add powdered sugar. Mix melted butter and melted chocolate, and add to first mixture. Add vanilla and the 8 crushed crackers, marshmallows, and nuts. Form a long roll or 2 short ones then roll in the extra crushed crumbs. Wrap in waxed paper, chill, and slice as needed.

Shortbread

1 cup butter
½ cup plus 2 tablespoons super-fine sugar
1 teaspoon vanilla
2 cups flour

Whip butter until light and fluffy. Gradually add sugar while continuing to beat. Add vanilla and flour gradually, beating well. Roll into balls (if too sticky chill 30 minutes). Bake at 275 degrees for 18 to 20 minutes.

Variation: ½ cup dark brown sugar could be substituted for super-fine sugar.

To Do or Not to Do
A Guide to Gracious Living

Etiquette is the art of gracious living each day, not just rules observed during special occasions. The concept of etiquette is to show respect and courtesy to those people with whom you come in contact with each day—be they family, friends, or dignitaries. Emerson said; "Time should never be too short for courtesy, because courtesy and good manners are the cornerstone upon which all workable rules of etiquette and protocol are built."

Dining

Gracious dining is a part of everyday life; it should not be kept just for company affairs. The do's and don'ts of correct table setting and service are founded on the comfort, pleasure, and courtesy of those seated at the table. It requires putting a few principles into practice that have become customs.

Napkins

Fancy napkin folding can be used as part of the table decoration, but the customary folding of napkins is a simple square or rectangle. The usual place for a napkin is at the left of the dinner fork with the fold facing away from the fork.

Glassware

The glassware used on the table should be placed about one inch from the tip of the knife. It remains on the table for the entire meal.

Dinnerware

The dinner or luncheon plate should be placed about one inch from the edge of the table. Choose a plate that best suits the meal being served.

Silverware

The customary practice in the placement of silver flatware is in the order that it is to be used, working from the outside toward the plate. Spoons and knives are at the right of the plate, with the sharp knife edge facing the plate in readiness for cutting. Forks are placed at the left of the plate, with tines up. The table will be lovelier if not more than three pieces of silverware are placed on each side of the plate at one time. It's customary to serve the dessert with the silver on the right of the plate where it is most convenient to use.

Seating

At home the mother and father are the host and hostess. A female guest of honor is always seated on the right of the host. A male guest of honor is always seated on the right of the hostess. The customary seats for host and hostess are at the ends or opposite sides of the table, with the hostess conveniently near the kitchen door. Serving the guest of honor first is considered proper.

Table Service

Never leave a vacant plate in front of a guest between courses. As one course is removed, immediately replace it with another course.

Place the salad plate at the left or directly above the dinner plate.

A hot beverage goes on the right, just below the water glass.

Bread-and-butter plates may be omitted at informal meals when buttered rolls are served. Hot breads should be served in a serving dish with a napkin folded around them.

All service is from the left except beverages, they are served from the right. Place and remove all dishes from the left, in which case the plate already in place is removed with the left hand, while next course is put in place with right hand.

Plates for crackers and cakes may have doilies.

Handle goblets by the stem and tumblers or glasses close to the bottom. Never lift a glass from the table to refill it except at very informal meals when water service is on the table.

When dessert is served, clear the table of everything except the centerpiece. If necessary, remove crumbs from the table with a folded napkin and a small plate. Additional silver needed for the course may now be put in place at the right, above or directly on the dessert plate.

Hostess Gift

It is a special honor to be invited to someone's home either as a house guest or to a dinner party. Show your appreciation by taking a hostess gift. The amount of the gift depends on the occasion. A bottle of your dried herbs, jam or jellies, candy, or a small plant make a nice dinner gift. Something more personal is appropriate for a house guest gift.

Wedding Receptions

Guest Book

A nice custom, but not mandatory, is the signing of names in a guest book. The guests sign the book with their formal names (Mr. and Mrs. Glen Gray—not Jack and Jill Jones). The book can ask for addresses for future reference and for sending thank you notes.

Reception

As you begin to pass through the receiving line give the first person in the line your name. All you have to say is "Hello, Jane is a beautiful bride" or "A lovely wedding." What you say to the bridal couple depends on how well you know them. Shake hands with the groom and say congratulations; shake hands with the bride or kiss her on the cheek if you know her well and wish her happiness. (Never congratulate her for securing a husband). Then move on quickly. You can chat later.

Introductions

We should not forget to make them! The basic rule to remember is that the person you mention first is the one you are honoring. "Mrs. White, this is Mrs. Green" or "Mary Brown I'd like you to meet John Jones." In the case of introducing a man to a woman, the woman's name is usually mentioned first. An exception to this is usually in business when a woman employee is presented to a male executive or in education a teacher or an administer is shown respect by mentioning the man's name first. "Mr. Redd this is a new student, Ann White."

When you are introducing members of the same sex, the guiding factors are age, rank, or degrees of distinction. Again the person to be honored is the first person mentioned.

"Sally Green, John Jones."
"Sally Green this is John Jones."
"Sally, this is John Jones, John, Sally Green."
More Formal Way:
"May I present—"
"May I introduce—"
"I should like to introduce—"
If you are not sure whether they are acquainted,
"Do you know—"
"Have you met—"
The best acknowledgment is,
"How do you do?"
"Hello" or "Hi" if they are your age.
You can reply,
"It's a pleasure to meet you."
"I'm glad to have the opportunity to meet you."
In business, "How do you do?"

Shaking hands is not as customary for women as it once was. A man always shakes hands with a man—he may nod to a woman and only shake hands if *she* offers. However, if someone offers a handshake, you should be ready to shake. A handshake should be brief, firm, and friendly.

A man will rise whenever he is introduced to a woman or a girl. A girl or woman does not rise unless introduced to an older woman, a much older man, or to honor a distinguished person. In your office you do not rise unless someone important comes to your desk to talk to you. It is not necessary for a man to stand up when you enter his office. Convenience overrules chivalry today in the business world.

Cleaning Up

Household Cleaning Tips and Hints

Furniture Wash and Beauty Treatment

3 tablespoons mineral oil
1 tablespoon turpentine
1 quart very hot water

Mix together in a tin can so you can discard when finished. Wipe on with a nylon stocking (cut open) and polish with a soft dry cloth.

Wood Furniture Polish

⅓ cup turpentine
⅓ cup white vinegar
⅓ cup mineral oil

Apply generously and wipe off with nylon stocking. Polish with a soft dry cloth.

Waxed Wood Furniture and Painted Cupboard Cleaner

3 tablespoons white vinegar
1 cup warm water

Apply with a clean soft cloth and wipe dry. This removes cloudiness on wood, and is a good in-between cleaner for wood.

Badly Soiled Painted Surface Cleaner

2 quarts hot water
¼ cup ammonia (non-sudsy)
¼ cup white vinegar
2 tablespoons super washing soda (Arm and Hammer)

Wash a small area at a time. Rinse with clear warm water.

Window and Mirror Cleaner

Use equal parts rubbing alcohol and water.
    OR
Use equal parts white vinegar and water.

All-Weather Window Cleaner

1 pint rubbing alcohol
1 tablespoon ammonia (nonsudsy)
1 tablespoon liquid detergent or white vinegar
1 pint water

Mix in a container and pour in a spray bottle. Prevents steaming and freezing.

Wall Cleaning Solution

½ cup vinegar
¼ cup baking soda
1 cup sudsy ammonia
1 gallon hot water

Wash up walls, not down.

Wood Paneling Cleaner

1 ounce olive oil or mineral oil
2 ounces white vinegar
1 quart warm water

Wipe paneling with cleaner and then wipe with a dry cloth.

Drain Cleaner

1 cup table salt
1 cup baking soda
1 cup white vinegar
2 quarts boiling water

Combine salt, soda, and vinegar and pour down drain followed by boiling water. Will unclog grease and soap residue.

Garbage Disposal Cleaner

½ cup vinegar

Freeze vinegar in ice cube tray and run through the garbage disposal.

Non–Self-Cleaning Oven Cleaner

½ cup clear household ammonia

Pour ammonia in a disposable pan and place in the oven overnight. Oven will wipe clean.

Note: If you have a gas oven, make sure you turn off the pilot light.

Oven Rack Cleaner

1 cup clear household ammonia

Soak several paper towels or an old terry cloth towel with ammonia. Place oven racks in a large garbage bag with the ammonia soaked paper towels or towel; seal bag tightly, place outside, and let stand overnight. Wash with hot soapy water.

Glass Oven Door Cleaner

Soak paper towels with clear ammonia. Wipe glass with ammonia and let stand for 3 to 4 hours, wipe with hot soapy water, and dry carefully.

Dishwasher

Keep dishwasher clean and fresh smelling and the drains unclogged by adding ½ cup white vinegar to the rinse cycle when you are washing glasses and plates only—not silverware or pans. Sprinkle 4 tablespoons baking soda across the bottom of the dishwasher every month to keep dishes sparkling.

Shower

Wipe shower with a squeegee after each use. Occasionally wipe shower and shower door down with undiluted white vinegar or lemon oil (be careful to not get on the chrome or shower floor). Let stand ½ hour or more. Rinse well.

Furniture Dusting

Use just enough oil or wax to absorb into the cloth to remove dust.

Do not mix the oil and wax in the same container. Do not use oil to dust waxed surfaces.

Keep dust cloths clean. After washing repeat above procedure.

Each time you clean a room, place a few drops of a fragrant oil on a light bulb or spray the room with a fresh potpourri scent to give the house a nice aroma.

Vinegar Household Uses

Frost-Free Windshields—Vinegar will help keep windshields ice and frost free. When a car has to be left outside overnight in the winter, coat the windshield with a solution of three parts white vinegar to one part water.

Eliminate White Moisture Ring on Wooden Furniture—Mix equal parts of white vinegar and olive oil and rub on white ring with the grain of the wood. Then polish. Always try on a small area first.

Longer Lasting Flowers—Combine 2 tablespoons vinegar, 3 tablespoons sugar, and 1 quart of water to place cut flowers in.

Remove Catsup Stain—Within 24 hours, spot the stained article with white vinegar; launder as usual. Also works well on carpet.

Reduce Skin Blemishes—Pat face with a cotton ball soaked in white vinegar.

Tenderize Meat—Rub a tough steak with equal parts of vinegar and olive oil, let stand for several hours.

Freshen Lunch Boxes—Dampen a piece of fresh bread with white vinegar and put it in the lunch box overnight.

Loosen Tough Stains or Lime Deposits or Discoloration—Boil ¼ cup white vinegar with two cups of water in a small glass, aluminum, or porcelain pan. Wash with hot soapy water.

Clean Electric Irons—Rub equal amounts of heated white vinegar and salt on the sole plate of the iron. Rub iron on a piece of scrap fabric.

Cleaner Clothes—Add about 1 cup of white vinegar to the final rinse in the washer to produce a more thorough rinse and de-static clothes. Good for washer as it cleans the hose and drain.

Eliminate Cooking Odors—Boil a tablespoon white vinegar mixed in a cup of water.

Cleaning Jars—Peanut butter or mayonnaise jars saved for storage can be rinsed with white vinegar before reusing them to lessen the odor of the former contents.

Painting Odors—Pour one cup white vinegar into a large flat glass container and place in painted area.

Bathtub and Sinks

Wipe bathtub and sinks with undiluted white vinegar and then sprinkle lightly with baking soda; clean with a sponge or cloth and then rinse well.

Formica Counter Tops

Wipe with a soft cloth soaked in undiluted white vinegar.

Bowl Cleaner

Clean and deodorize toilet bowl by pouring ½ cup white vinegar into the bowl and letting it stand for 5 minutes; brush and flush. If stubborn stains remain, spray with vinegar and brush vigorously. For badly stained bowls pour ½ cup Cola in the bowl and let stand for 5 minutes; brush and flush.

Treated Wood Floors, Linoleum, or Carpet

Damp mop wood floors and linoleum with 1 cup white vinegar and ½ gallon warm water. Wipe carpets with a terry cloth towel soaked in diluted white vinegar and wrung out well. Spot carpets with undiluted white vinegar; scrub carefully with a toothbrush, then wipe dry.

For animal stains in carpet or upholstery, wash area with club soda or white vinegar and blot dry with paper towels or terry cloth towel. Stand on towels to bring up moisture.

Vinegar Pie

    4 eggs
    1½ cups sugar
    ¼ cup butter or margarine, melted
    1½ tablespoons cider or white vinegar
    1 teaspoon vanilla
    1 nine-inch unbaked pie shell

Preheat oven to 350 degrees. Combine eggs, sugar, butter, vinegar, and vanilla and mix well. Pour into pie shell and bake 50 minutes or until firm. Cool on wire rack and serve with chopped nuts or whipped cream.

Baking Soda Household Uses

Remove Odors from Chopping Boards—Sprinkle dry baking soda on a damp sponge and rub; rinse with clear water.

Remove Odors from Plastic Containers—Soak overnight in a baking soda and water solution.

Cleaning Chrome Fixtures—Sprinkle baking soda on a damp sponge and gently scour; rinse and buff dry.

Sweet-Smelling Clothes—Add ½ cup baking soda to the rinse cycle. Sprinkle baking soda on dirty clothes in hamper.

Bleach Booster—Add ½ cup baking soda with half the usual amount of liquid chlorine bleach. Clothes get just as clean with less bleach odor.

Freshen Car Carpeting—Sprinkle baking soda lightly on carpeting, wait 15 minutes, and vacuum. Remember under floor mats and in trunk of the car.

Household Hints

Freeze whole walnuts before cracking. They will come out whole instead of broken.

Freeze cranberries before grinding. Frozen berries hold their juice.

Sprinkle potato flakes in soup to help absorb liquid. Its easier for a small child to eat. Tasty too.

Oil a cup or measuring spoon before measuring molasses or peanut butter, the contents will slip out easily making it easier to wash the cup or spoon.

A piece of an apple or an orange placed in the jar with dry, hard brown sugar will soften it and make it moist again. Remove the apple or orange after 24 hours if the jar is kept tightly covered. The sugar will remain soft.

Save the spiced vinegar from sweet pickles (or any pickles for that matter) in a glass jar. Use for pepping up salad dressings or to marinate potatoes for a potato salad.

Hold the seasoning! When you're making soup, do not add onion or vegetable seasonings until the very last. Otherwise the flavor goes up in steam.

Vegetables that grow underground should be covered when being cooked. Those that are grown above the ground should be left uncovered.

When a recipe calls for a sharp-flavored cheese, a mild cheese may be substituted by clever use of seasoning. Add a little dry mustard, a little pepper, and a dash of Worcestershire Sauce. Even experts never guess your deep secret.

Sprinkle granulated sugar over that meringue-topped pie and watch how easily it cuts.

After baking a pumpkin pie, set it on a cake cooler. The bottom crust will always be dry.

A small pan of water underneath gingerbread, when it is baking, is an effective way to prevent it from burning.

Place several marbles in the kettle when making chili, preserves, apple butter, or anything that requires continued stirring. Marbles will roll constantly across the bottom to prevent sticking.

Those provoking yellow stains that occur in the bathroom basin can be removed easily. Mix together a small amount of peroxide and equal proportions of cream of tartar, then rub thoroughly.

Use a new metal pot cleaner to rub the skin off new potatoes or carrots, they are just rough enough to rub off the outer skin without wasting the body.

289

To remove ball point pen stains from clothing, use hair spray or rubbing alcohol to wash the spot.

Baking pie shells on lowest rack will make them lighter and crisper.

Add a little sugar to celery or carrots when cooking to insure crispness.

Place spray starch on white tennis shoes before you wear them so the dirt won't grind into the shoes.

Liquor Substitutions

For dry (unsweet) red wine in soups and entrees:
Water
Beef broth, bouillon, or consommé
Tomato juice (plain or diluted)
Diluted cider vinegar
Diluted red wine vinegar
Liquid drained from canned mushrooms

For dry (unsweet) white wine in soups and entrees:
Water
Chicken broth, bouillon, or consommé
Ginger ale
White grape juice
Diluted cider vinegar
Diluted white wine vinegar
Liquid drained from canned mushrooms

In cheese dishes (i.e., fondue, rarebit, etc.):
Chicken broth
White grape juice
Ginger ale

In desserts:

    Brandy: apple cider, peach, or apricot syrup

    Rum: pineapple juice, syrup flavored with almond or Rum extract

    Sherry: orange juice, pineapple juice

    Kirsch: syrup or juice from black cherries, raspberries, boysenberries, currants, or grapes; cherry cider

    Cognac: juice from peaches, apricots, or pears

    Cointreau: fresh orange juice, frozen orange juice concentrate

    Creme de menthe: spearmint extract, oil, or spearmint diluted with a little water or grapefruit juice

    Red burgundy: grape juice

    White burgundy: white grape juice

    Champagne: ginger ale

    Claret: grape juice, current juice or syrup, cherry cider

Note: To cut the sweetness of the syrups, dilute with water. The only substitute that might be used for flaming desserts is a sugar cube soaked in lemon extract set on top of dessert and ignited.

Appendix
Handy Kitchen Chart

Kitchen Math with Metric Tables

Measure	Equivalent	Metric (ML)
1 tablespoon	3 teaspoons	14.8 milliliters
2 tablespoons	1 ounce	29.6 milliliters
¼ cup	4 tablespoons	59.2 milliliters
⅓ cup	5 tablespoons, plus 1 teaspoon	78.9 milliliters
½ cup	8 tablespoons	118.4 milliliters
1 cup	16 tablespoons	236.8 milliliters
1 pint	2 cups	473.6 milliliters
1 quart	4 cups	947.2 milliliters
1 liter	4 cups, plus 3⅓ tablespoons	1,000.0 milliliters
1 ounce (dry)	2 tablespoons	28.35 grams
1 pound	16 ounces	453.59 grams
2.21 pounds	35.3 ounces	1.00 kilogram

Candy Syrup Temperatures
without a Thermometer

A ½ teaspoonful of syrup dropped into fresh cold water:

Thread (230°–234°)	Spins a soft 3-inch thread
Soft Ball (234°–240°)	Forms a ball, when pressed together, but does not hold its shape
Firm Ball (242°–248°)	Forms a ball that holds its shape
Hard Ball (250°–268°)	Forms a hard, but plastic, ball
Soft Crack (270°–290°)	Forms hard, but not brittle, thread
Hard Crack (300°–310°)	Forms hard, brittle thread that breaks when pressed

When the recipe calls for:	You can use:
1 tablespoon cornstarch	2 tablespoons all-purpose flour (for thickening)
1 whole egg	2 egg yolks plus 1 tablespoon water
1 cup homogenized milk	1 cup skim milk plus 2 tablespoons butter or margarine OR: ½ cup evaporated milk plus ½ cup water
1 ounce unsweetened chocolate	3 tablespoons cocoa powder plus 1 tablespoon butter or margarine
1 teaspoon baking powder	½ teaspoon cream of tartar plus ¼ teaspoon baking soda
1 cup sifted cake flour	⅞ cup sifted all-purpose flour (⅞ cup is 1 cup *less* 2 Tbsp.)
½ cup (1 stick) butter or margarine	7 tablespoons vegetable shortening
1 cup soured milk or buttermilk	1 tablespoon white vinegar plus sweet milk to equal 1 cup

1 clove fresh garlic	1 teaspoon garlic salt OR ⅛ teaspoon garlic powder
2 teaspoons minced onion	1 teaspoon onion powder
1 tablespoon finely chopped fresh chives	1 teaspoon freeze-dried chives
1 teaspoon dry leaf herb	1 tablespoon chopped fresh herbs
1 cup dairy sour cream	1 tablespoon lemon juice plus evaporated milk to make 1 cup

When the recipe calls for: You start with:

When the recipe calls for:	You start with:
5½ cups cooked fine noodles	8 ounce package fine noodles
4 cups sliced raw potatoes	4 medium-size potatoes
2½ cups sliced carrots	1 pound raw carrots
4 cups shredded cabbage	1 small cabbage (1 pound)
1 teaspoon grated lemon rind	1 medium-size lemon
2 tablespoons lemon juice	1 medium-size lemon
4 teaspoons grated orange rind	1 medium-size orange
4 cups sliced apples	4 medium-size apples
2 cups shredded Swiss or Cheddar cheese	8-ounce piece Swiss or Cheddar cheese
1 cup soft bread crumbs	2 slices fresh bread
1 cup egg whites	6 or 7 large eggs
1 cup egg yolks	11 or 12 large eggs
4 cups chopped walnuts or pecans	1 pound shelled walnuts or pecans

Index

About the Authors

Patricia Hemming

Maurine Humphris

Patricia Hemming is a graduate of the University of Utah in Home Economics and has worked as a Home Economist for Mountain Fuel and the Coordinator of Householder Education for Utah Power. She is currently a consultant for national advertising firms and a freelance writer. She lives in Layton, Utah, with her husband, Michael, and their daughter Keely.

Maurine Humphris is a graduate of Utah State University in Home Economics Education and served as the Program Specialist for Family and Consumer Science for the Utah State Office of Education. She and her husband, Joe, live in South Ogden, Utah.

Both authors are popular lecturers on the role of traditions in families.

9 26575 76623 6